The long c

C000131995

The long and the short of it

… reflections on reality in different measures

John L. Bell

Wild Goose Publications
Wild Goose Resource Group

Copyright © 2022 WGRG, Iona Community, Glasgow

Published 2022 by
Wild Goose Publications
Suite 9, Fairfield, 1048 Govan Road, Glasgow G51 4XS, Scotland
the publishing division of the Iona Community.
Scottish Charity No. SC003794. Limited Company Reg. No. SC096243.
www.ionabooks.com

ISBN 978-1-80432-006-8
Cover image © Dan Talson | Dreamstime.com

**The publishers gratefully acknowledge the support of the Drummond Trust,
3 Pitt Terrace, Stirling FK8 2EY in producing this book.**

All rights reserved. No part of this publication may be reproduced in any form
or by any means, including photocopying, electronic publishing or any
information storage or retrieval system, without written permission from the
Wild Goose Resource Group at wildgoose@wildgoose.scot

John L. Bell has asserted his right in accordance with the Copyright, Designs
and Patents Act, 1988, to be identified as the author of this work.

Overseas distribution
Australia: Willow Connection Pty Ltd, 1/13 Kell Mather Drive,
Lennox Head NSW 2478
New Zealand: Pleroma, Higginson Street, Otane 4170, Central Hawkes Bay

Printed by Bell & Bain, Thornliebank, Glasgow

Contents

Introduction

This book was intended to be a collection of short reflections, mostly featured on Radio 4's *Thought for the Day*. These, for the most part, deal with issues of current interest with the intention of allowing for their consideration from a faith perspective. They have to be short – 2 minutes 40 seconds – which is appropriate for some subjects, but dangerous when matters of magnitude are reduced to sound bites

The Long and the Short of It emerged to enable a more comprehensive consideration of bigger issues. The range is very wide – from pandemic to paedophilia, from death to discrimination. None of the long items deal with easy issues. Most of them have not been the subject of religious discourse, because they are either contentious or embarrassing. But I believe that neither I nor anyone else has any right to preach or speak on matters of easy agreement if we are not also prepared to deal with what is awkward or contentious.

My understanding of the Christian faith is rooted in the belief that all the created universe and the myriad endeavours of humanity exist in the interest and under the aegis of God. Therefore even closed doors sometimes need to be opened, and favoured attitudes re-examined.

John L. Bell
February 2022

Acknowledgements

I am indebted to the Department of Religion in the BBC for the invitation to present *Thought for the Day*, and to Greenbelt Festival for the privilege of giving the seminars on which most of the longer items are based. I also acknowledge resultant correspondence from listeners which has confirmed and challenged my own assumptions in equal measure.

I am particularly indebted to the magnificent work of Sandra Kramer of Wild Goose Publications whose care and industry have enabled texts intended for speaking to become suitable for reading. Working during the pandemic must have been arduous enough without having to deal with my misspellings, colloquialisms and extraneous verbiage.

Telling the truth

One of the sad behavioural phenomena of recent years has been the increase of vitriol, including even death threats, directed at public figures by people who disagree with what they have to say. This used to happen mostly in the case of elected politicians, but it now affects schoolchildren like Greta Thunberg for raising environmental concerns, or medical experts such as Anthony Fauci for advising the wearing of masks; and at the weekend the philanthropist Bill Gates revealed that he was being demonised for encouraging preventative vaccination.

I've been trying to identify the reasons behind the vindictive nature of the invective directed at these people.

I think that one possibility is a fear of the power wielded by unaccountable individuals. I certainly share this apprehension. For there are a number of prominent unelected people, mostly men, whose wealth exceeds the GDP of small nations and whose tentacles of influence, whether in relation to social media or to the spread of industrial power, stretch around the globe.

But Thunberg and Fauci are certainly not in this category.

Another possible reason is the prevalence of fake news – something both condemned and propagated by certain populist politicians. Fake news can encourage people to doubt the truth about issues concerning which a proportion of the general public is passionate.

But it might all come down to the fact that truth is not always popular or comfortable, especially if it challenges long-held assumptions or comes with a cost.

If the Christian faith has any light to shed on this, it would be a perception which is not specific to that tradition, namely that the hallmark of what is true should be that it is liberating rather than constricting; it should shed light rather than conserve ignorance.

The maxim Jesus articulates is, 'You shall know the truth and the truth shall set you free.'

At one time it was claimed that the brains of black people were smaller than those of whites, that punishment was a possible remedy for dyslexia and autism in children, that rape was an offence encouraged by women, that people who spoke minority languages were uncultured.

Challenging these prejudices with the truth was never a popular activity. But to acknowledge the truth is liberating both for the oppressed and for their oppressors.

Thought for the Day
20 June 2020

Light at the end of the tunnel
... a reflection on the Corona crisis

For many people, the current Covid 19 pandemic has suffused our life and conversation in a way nothing else has. It has dominated the news; it has disrupted work, public worship, schooling, and family and community life. It has required us to change our transportation and shopping habits, stalled leisure activities, and changed our visual appearance because of the need to wear masks. It might even have made us afraid to spend time with people we meet in the street.

There is and will be for a long time much discussion and analysis of this crisis from medical, political and sociological perspectives. I want to discuss it from a faith perspective. However, my starting point is not theology but palliative care.

Palliative care

In using the term 'palliative care', I am not referring to the medical assistance and pastoral or spiritual support given to people who are dying or bereft. I'm talking about the plenitude of saccharine piety which churches have been offering to people in response to the pandemic. Sucking a pastille might temporarily soothe a sore throat; but it's a palliative and not a cure, especially if the throat is affected by cancer.

I believe people need more than saccharine piety. This need is not a new thing. It confronted a friend of mine, a Roman Catholic priest in Ireland, when on 27th December 2004 he was celebrating mass for an enclosed order of nuns. After the eucharist, as he was bidding goodbye to the assembly, one of them – a normally quiet and friendly 80-year-old sister – turned on him and said, 'What did God think he was up to on St Stephen's Day?'

St Stephen's Day is always 26th December and in 2004 it was the day a tsunami devastated parts of South Asia.

Whether it is a tsunami or a pandemic, both of which are indiscriminate in the range of people affected, it is right that the church should offer that kind of consolation which is called the 'comfort of religion'. People need to know God's love mediated through sensitive care, well-chosen words, scripture and the sacraments. Believers need to be reminded that nothing in the heights or the depths can separate them from the love of God which is in Christ Jesus.

With all of this I concur, and applaud people who are finding appropriate words for this long season of bewilderment. I do not exempt myself from pastoral engagement, but I do not believe that this is all that faith has to offer. The old nun's question – 'What was God up to?' – haunts me.

In considering how faith responds, I want to look at three possible trajectories:

1   A vocabulary for lament

2   A theological critique of the pandemic

3   Hopeful potentials

1. LAMENT

I received an email last June from a church musician who was enquiring as to what people might sing which would allow for an articulation of their feelings of anxiety and distress. There wasn't anything which immediately came to her mind. Was that perhaps because such expressions go against the grain of Christian Positivism, or is it that we lack a vocabulary to give voice to it?

It took me back to an evening, now sixteen years ago, in Minneapolis when I treated three younger colleagues to a theatrical event which I had seen before they were conceived. The name of the show was *Hair*. I saw it when I was twenty-one.

I can still sing some of its short songs. I remember its multicultural cast, their psychedelic clothes and the then scandalous thirty seconds of full nudity on stage.

What I had forgotten, until I saw it again, was that this was a musical protesting against the Vietnam War. The central character was a young male hippy who, unlike others, decided not to flee the draft by going to Canada, but to leave his commune, join the military and be sent to fight in Vietnam where he was killed.

It came to the end of the performance. The audience rose to cheer an excellent production and cast. Then one of the minor characters came to the apron of the stage and motioned for silence. He said:

'We are so glad to be playing to you tonight in Minneapolis.

'Just today, we discovered that the first female in the US military to be killed in the current Gulf War came from this city. We also discovered that there is a fund established in her memory. The money from it is going to look after Iraqi children who have been orphaned or wounded by allied bombing.

'So after each performance we are going to stand outside with buckets as you leave. If you wish, you can make a donation to this fund to help these desolate children in Iraq.'

And then from this predominantly adult audience came the sound of weeping. This was at a time when the Patriot Act forbade public criticism of the government and when songs by a female band called the Dixie Chicks had been pulled from public performance.

This anti-Vietnam-war musical from the '60s voiced protest and lament which no contemporary musical in 2004 would have been allowed to do in the USA. And in donating to a fund set up in memory of a local girl who had been killed in Iraq, people were making perhaps the first tangible sign of their discontent with a war then in its second of eight years.

Protest and lament – '60s, South Africa & spirituals

In the '60s and '70s there was a vocabulary given to the public by artistes to articulate their rawness of feeling, not just songs which promised better days by and by. There were critical songs, like those of Bob Dylan berating the 'Masters of war', and of Pete Seeger who queried 'Where have all the flowers gone?'

Protest and lament are very old traditions. They were important in the struggle against apartheid in South Africa, articulated by the voices of a people who sang out their belief that things had to change as forcibly as they sang out their pain.

The national anthem of those under apartheid was not *Nkosi Sikelel' iAfrica* – that was a pan-African song. No, the anthem of those who suffered was much shorter – one word per verse:

Senzenina – What have we done wrong?
Sonosetu – What is our sin?

The text didn't come from a Hollywood lyricist, it came from the Bible. It appears in the first book of Samuel where David, whose life was threatened by King Saul, turns to Saul's son Jonathan and says:

What have I done wrong?
What is my sin?
(I Sam 20:1)

Psalms

But, of course, those of us who have some allegiance to the Jewish or Christian traditions shouldn't need to go to America or Africa for a vocabulary to articulate pain, anger, disappointment, frustration, victimisation. It's all there in the Psalms if only we can see beyond those used primarily for palliative care. Much as I love it, Psalm 23 is not a panacea.

Two years ago I was working on a book about the Psalms – not a commentary, but a series of reflections and insights which resulted from discussions with a whole range of people. I was most amazed by how some individuals took to Psalm 88, the bleakest in the Bible, which has accusations against God, questions to God, and sarcastic remarks about God. Time and again people recognised that it offered a vocabulary for those who were stuck for words because life was so hellish and praise songs weren't doing the trick.

Those encouraged by it included a girl whose brother had committed suicide, a woman in a predominantly impoverished Catholic parish in North Glasgow whose life had gone through the mill, and priests in an Anglican diocese which was riven and disputatious. Something in these angry words, offered to God, allowed for an honesty of expression which God permits but which polite faith regards as inadmissible.

Here, as another example, is a contemporary version of words from Psalm 77:

1. *I cry to God and he hears me;*
   in my times of trouble I seek him.
   By night my hands plead in prayer
   but I find nothing for my comfort.

2. *I think of God and I moan,*
   I meditate and feel useless.

> *God keeps the sleep from my eyes*
> *and my speech is lost in confusion.*

> 3. *I thought of days gone by*
>   *and remembered times now vanished;*
>   *I spent the night in deep distress*
>   *while my spirit murmured within me:*

> 4. *'Has God forgotten to be gracious?*
>   *Has anger doused his compassion?*
>   *Has God's mighty arm lost its grasp?*
>   *Does it hang powerless beside him?'* [1]

If you are asking yourself 'Where's the light at the end of the tunnel?' this might just be a glimmer. We in the church have no right to withhold from each other a vocabulary of lament which might enable us to release the anger, frustration and powerlessness that people feel within them. In the worst of times it is often a source of solidarity to realise that someone has been there before you.

Indeed, I wonder if we have any right to expect people to sing Hallelujah if we never offer the opportunity to ask, 'How long?'

2. THEOLOGY

I am interested in what theological understandings we share about the global pandemic, because I have not heard very much articulated. I suppose there are two polarities which to me are equally unattractive.

Sin-sniffing and escapism

At the one end of the spectrum we have the sin-sniffers, people who enjoy identifying iniquity in the same way as some individuals enjoy bad health. 'It all comes down to guilt and sin,' is what they would claim. It goes right back to the fall and to the inherited congenital moral malformation called 'original sin'.

Exactly what the iniquity is, however, is not identified. To say that the pandemic is caused by sin is wholly insufficient. Is it personal sin or corporate sin? Has it a root, a source, a furtive intention? Or is it the work of the Devil, who – as in the case of Job – has been given free rein by God to visit hardship on innocent people to test their fidelity?

At the other end of the theological, liturgical and emotional spectra are those who offer sentimental greeting-card nostrums or who – as in some parts of America – believe that the virus won't affect those who keep praising the Lord. This may be an attractive displacement activity, as long as you don't fall prey to Covid 19, but it is a fruitless escape from reality.

I find neither of these caricatured extremes satisfying. But what do you say to explain an unjust and all-pervasive threat?

I want to offer three perspectives which I don't imagine will be popular; but I believe they should at least be aired.

a) Finitude

What we are dealing with as regards the global pandemic is not just a menacing disease but our own finitude. Just as some people shy away from engaging with those who have a mental or physical disability because – if they are honest – they don't know what to say or do, so in the face of a global pandemic we are lost for words and a failsafe response. This is not a broken leg which will heal, or a cancer which might respond to chemotherapy. We can't say with any certainty to people who suspect they have the disease, 'I'm sure you'll be all right.'

We are confronted with an invisible agent which all the wealth, military might and accrued knowledge of experts has been unable to quickly exterminate or tame.

We are confronted with our own finitude. We are not gods. And that is easier to say than it is to believe. It is the dilemma of Job which neither his sense of righteousness nor his comforters' convictions regarding sin are able to fathom.

In the West we subconsciously believe (though on what basis?) that this current plague shouldn't be happening to us. Exceptionalism has bogus roots in theology.

Hawaii

Some years ago I was working in Hawaii, in Hilo, the big island. One day those of us who were not native islanders were taken up to an observation point near the rim of an active volcano. A local man explained that if and when the volcano threatened eruption, it was important to establish the likely direction of the lava flow so that people could move out of their houses.

It struck me that if I lived on that island, I wouldn't consider living anywhere apart from the coast, given the possibility of a volcanic eruption. But the islanders didn't think that way. For them, risk and uncertainty are givens you have to live with. For most Western urbanites, risk and uncertainty are what we try to avoid.

At the core of this, especially for people of the Judaeo-Christian tradition, is a common misreading of Genesis chapter 1.

In that great creation hymn, there is a constant refrain:

God saw that it was good. (Gen 1:4)

At the end of the creation cycle the approval rating is higher:

God saw all that he had made,
and it was very good. (Gen 1:31)

Good … but NOT perfect.
  Indeed very good … but NOT perfect.

It is not that creation has a moral defect, but that it has fault lines – of which the San Andreas fault in California is among the best known. Creation has logical inconsistencies, as when some Australian gum trees burst into flame not for the purpose of extermination, but as a means of germination.

Invincible nations

The nations which believe they are invincible have the most difficulty in dealing with menacing, untameable threats. We know what to do should our country be the object of a trade embargo or invasive enemy surveillance. We can use our power, our ingenuity to deal with this. But we have no immediate defence against threats to our existence which come from a world we presume to be perfect and predictable rather than good but imperfect.

We have to learn that we are not invincible gods but vulnerable mortals, living in a world which is sometimes arrhythmic, often from natural causes but increasingly because of human interference. No one I have ever met in the developing world has difficulty in accepting that life and risk are conjoined. But Westerners are prone to believe they are entitled to a pain-free existence.

b) The relationship between humanity and the earth

We will all have heard, based on scripture, that God has given dominion over the earth – dominion but not domination. There is an integrity in creation which is not ours to alter, and so we have to live with it in a symbiotic relationship.

We were alerted to this in Scotland when some years ago a mining conglomerate offered to fell a mountain on the island of Harris and dig a huge quarry to extract stone to be shattered into aggregate for road-building. I'd love to discuss the issue in detail, but this is not the occasion.

What I want to allude to is the government inquiry at which proponents and opponents of the plan presented their cases. Among the opponents were two very different men. One was large and dressed in the robes and headgear of a Canadian First Nations leader. He was Chief Stone Eagle of the Mi'kmaq nation. The other, a much slighter figure, was a native of Harris, a Gaelic speaker and a professor of theology, Donald MacLeod. Their objections were on remarkably similar grounds.

Donald MacLeod's was the more biblical, and one of his stunning observations was that we bond quickly with the notion that humankind is mandated to 'till the earth' *(Genesis 2:15)*. However Donald pointed out that the word 'till' was more commonly translated from the Hebrew as 'serve'.

The Bible bears witness to the need for a right relationship between humankind and the planet we inhabit. The story of Noah has God throw into the sky his bow. The bow, especially when called the rainbow, was not intended as a symbol of Gay Pride but an emblem of war. God's weapon of mass destruction was never again to be used to annihilate the natural world. Humankind, however, did not make a similar covenant with the earth, and so it is the prophets and the poets who use graphic language to alert the human race to how its own existence depends on living in a complementary relationship with nature. Thus:

Jeremiah: *Your wrongdoing has upset nature's order*
            and your sins have kept away her bounty.
            (Jer 5:25)

Haggai: *It is your fault that the heavens withhold*
            their moisture and the earth its produce.
            (Hag 1:10)

Isaiah: *The earth lurches like a drunkard,*
            the sins of its inhabitants weigh heavy on it.

It falls to rise no more.
(Is 24:20)

Few theologians have dealt with this intrinsic relationship between humanity and the natural order. One reason for our gross neglect in this matter is that it is only recently, post the industrial revolution, that nature has begun to affect us negatively. Rather than re-establish a proper relationship, we go for mastery rather than servanthood.

The agrochemical industry will produce better fertilisers; the pharmacological industry will produce better vaccines. Highly commendable but sticking plasters on a running sore. We need to learn servanthood, not mastery.

A World Health Organization team has recently been investigating the source of Covid 19 in a wet market in Wuhan, China. One credible suggestion is that something went amiss with regard to the transgressing of boundaries between the animal and human kingdoms.

We need to learn servanthood, not mastery; relationship rather than domination.

There is a third theological perspective which is closely related. I'm going to call it:

c) The omnipresent temptation of self-induced myopia

In less stilted language, I mean the all-pervasive attraction of selfishness.

It is surely evident to all that this pandemic has inspired amazing altruism in a whole range of people. The sacrificial commitment of many in the health and caring services cannot be underestimated, and some of the most unexpected people have been drawn into a nationwide web of healing.

But the sound of public applause for those on the front line ringing from street to street has long since died. The weariness of a nation unable to deal with a continuous disruption to normal living has resulted in expressions of selfishness replacing those of gratitude.

It has been particularly evident among the wealthy and privileged ...

... politicians and their personal advisers claiming exemption from the constraints imposed on others; and outsourcing essential services to parties favourable to the government.

... those with access to private jet travel flying off to regions forbidden to those who use public airlines.

... British holiday-makers in Switzerland fleeing from their hotels to avoid having to undergo quarantine.

... the constant bragging about post-Brexit Britain being both global and world-beating (two terms constituting an oxymoron) as if dealing with the pandemic were a race for Olympic victory rather than a cooperative effort.

... the inability of commercial property owners – perhaps the only class of people with a guaranteed income – to share the pain of their tenants who cannot pay the rent because of restricted income or joblessness.

None of this smacks of altruism. It is, rather, evidence that avarice and selfishness are alive and well. And I believe that it has to be named, in order that there might be repentance.

One of the missing words in popular parlance in the past year – despite all the talk about our having to deal with an enemy or being on a war footing – has been sacrifice, particularly on the part of the privileged.

It might be that it sounds too religious, or unpalatable, but I believe that it is essential that the people of our nations, and especially those who are Christian, recognise that sacrifice is not just what is expected of workers in the medical, care and essential service industries. As in a war, it should be expected of us all.

The question is not 'How much can I avoid?' but 'How and where can I contribute?'

I have a modest salary. But in the last year I have saved a great deal of money. I have bought very few new items of clothing or household furnishing, I haven't been on holiday, and I haven't patronised restaurants or cafes whose workers depend on customers coming through the door.

The moment I realised this, two prospects dawned on me: I could either feel very fortunate and self-satisfied, or I could take the opportunity to show the kind of generosity which I could not normally afford. It seemed to me that not to consider lightening the load of others – whether they be individuals or charities – was to opt for self-aggrandisement over solidarity.

I tend to think that you and I know what Jesus and the prophets would have recommended.

3. HOPEFUL POTENTIALS

Now we come to what might be more clearly considered as light at the end of the tunnel.

Renewed valuing of the incarnation

There is a theological perspective grounded in a belief that in no small way led to the evangelisation of Scotland courtesy of the Irish monks led by Columba.

Imagine yourself living in Benbecula or Sutherland in the 5th century. Your existence is always precarious. You could die at any time in a number of ways of which we know little today:

- As at the time of Jesus, one in three children might die at birth, and one in four women might die giving birth.
- If the harvest fails, there is no other food source.

- If there is an epidemic among cattle or humans, there are no vaccines.
- If a fishing boat capsizes, there is no air-sea rescue.
- If you grow old (i.e. over forty) and have no children to care for you, your last years might be your worst.
- If you are a coastal people, you risk invasion, plundering and murder by Vikings.

As for a God ... oh you believe in one ... but this God is above the sky, remote from the exigencies of existence. And you fear that God every time thunder or disaster strikes.

And then you hear what seems profoundly unbelievable, that into such a risky world and uncertain existence God has come in person. And this person, called Jesus, has not been exempt from the exigencies of existence.

He has risked disease by touching people who are diseased.

He has relied on the charity of others and had no permanent home.

He has sailed on seas where had his friends not alerted him, he might have drowned.

He has been the victim of continual persecution and five attempts have been made on his life.

He has been put to death by the soldiers of an alien army and yet he has come back to life to prove that death is not the ultimate defeat.

And then you discover that this God, who is fully present in Jesus, has entered into complete solidarity with vulnerable people in an imperfect world, and has done this not out of anger or spite for those he created, but out of love, like the unconditional love a mother has for a child.

The incarnation is not about God pulling us out of the boat in stormy weather but about God getting into the boat beside us.

This, for me, is an ultimate consolation.

The reassessment of values

There can be few people who have not in some way discovered, over the past year, the hidden value in ordinary things. One such is the joy of human company, which previously we may well have taken for granted. I reckon that personally I have become a lot more appreciative of my friends and a lot more committed to them in the past year than in previous decades.

I have spent hours on phone calls where I would usually only devote five minutes. I've gone for long walks with people I have never journeyed with before. I have written letters to and received messages from people not just expressing concern for each other's welfare, but affection for the blessings of companionship ... in contrast to which Zoom meetings (unless between friends) can be more taxing than rewarding. This, to use a rare phrase I borrow from Mrs Thatcher, should lead us to 'Rejoice!'

We have also, many of us, become more attentive to the beauty and processes of the natural world, identifying both its novelty and the humanly contrived enemies to the wellbeing of nature. People look for birds in their neighbourhood whose song or chirps they have only just noticed. Or they learn the names of flowers and trees they only glanced at before. Or they begin to turn over ground they had never dug before.

This last has been my experience. I moved into my present house two years ago. It has a front garden the size of two bedsheets and was hitherto covered with red chips. Last year I had them lifted and turned over soil which hadn't seen sunlight for fifty years. I planted a dozen or so Maris Pipers which were sprouting in my pantry because I had forgotten to eat them, and in time they began to grow.

Many people in West Princes Street had never seen potatoes growing in a front garden. One woman marvelled at the purple and orange flowers on them and asked what I was growing. I said,

'Cannabis' and she replied, 'Tell me when it's ready!'

When they were ready for cropping I gave some to my Chinese neighbours upstairs who had never seen dirty potatoes before. Hitherto – as urbanites – they had always bought washed potatoes and therefore assumed that they, like other large vegetables – aubergine, squash etc – grew above ground.

Other people have made life decisions about lowering their intake of animal products because they want to reduce the amount of methane produced by cows, pigs and sheep. Others have decreased their use of materials which are not recyclable. Others have discovered improvements in health by walking or cycling, developing an exercise regime and generally taking more personal responsibility for their health and wellbeing.

These are all positives … and none of them would have flourished so beneficially if this pandemic had not occurred. These are glimmers of long-term hope which we should celebrate.

The new normal

The last book in the Bible, variously called Revelation or the Apocalypse, promises a new heaven and a new earth. We can pray for that but we also can begin to reconfigure the terrestrial component.

The Gospel, it seems to me, is not about conservation but about transformation, which was precisely the reason for the unpopularity of Jesus among those in his day who wanted a stable normality. But the purpose of God in history as witnessed by Jesus and the prophets is that everything – including normality – is to be changed and made new. There has perhaps only been one other occasion in the last eighty years when we have had the opportunity to envision a different future.

The last time was during the Second World War. In the middle stages of the war, the Anglican Archbishop of York, William Temple, convened a meeting of thinking people – including the poet and academic TS Eliot, and the author Dorothy Sayers – at Malvern in Worcestershire, with the express intention of encouraging innovative thinking with regard to post-war British society.

Temple was friendly with the then Home Secretary, William (later Lord) Beveridge, with whom he shared some of the ideas generated by the Malvern conference, and thus helped to shape the post-war agenda for the Welfare State, one prime component of which was the creation of the National Health Service.

The present Westminster government was not elected to deal with a pandemic, let alone rebuild the country post-pandemic. We don't tend to choose potential members of parliament on the basis of their creative or imaginative potentials. We tend to go for safe pairs of hands to keep the ship of state on course.

So who is going to think both prophetically and realistically about the future? Or are we just keen to get back to normal? … in which case we should ponder what the old normal was like.

Do we want to go back to believing that the only people who are important are the high-wage-earners, while the lowest-paid attendants in care homes, security people and delivery agents are called heroes but have to live on subsistence earnings?

Do we want to go back to the old normal where we thought that our health and social welfare services were thoroughly British, until we realised that of the first twelve frontline doctors to die from Covid 19, all but one were born in our former colonies?

Do we want to go back to the closure and sale of school playing fields and the underfunding and demotion in importance of the arts in secondary education?

Do we want to get back to over-polluted cities, high use of personal motorised transportation and a neglect of the countryside?

Do we want to return to a belief that we are a self-sufficient nation, when so much of our industrial base, our food production, our consumer goods, is dependent on trade with the very nations we either withdraw from or belittle?

Do we want to continue to see a social injustice having a better chance of being taken seriously and corrected not when a responsible authority or expert raises the issue, but when a celebrity does?

What will deliver us from the new normal being a slimmed down and stitched-up version of the failed old normal is not, I believe, in the gift of politicians. In this situation there needs to be a re-envisioning of the kind of nation we want to be and creative endeavour to establish the fundamentals necessary for the common good.

And this is an activity in which people of faith should be fully engaged as those who believe in light rather than darkness, cooperation rather than competition, generosity rather than selfishness. We should want all things to be made new rather than returning to 'normal'.

The light at the end of the tunnel is more likely to be discovered from below than bestowed on us from above.

In this context we might note the wisdom of a South African politician who, in the darkest days for his nation, said that if we cannot see the light at the end of the tunnel, it is not because there is no light. It is probably because the tunnel is not straight.

The above is a reconstruction of a Zoom lecture given for Jesuit communities in Edinburgh and Liverpool in February and March 2021.

---

[1] Psalm 77 copyright WGRG The Iona Community. Text as featured in *When Grief is Raw* (Wild Goose Publications) and recorded on the CD *The Last Journey* (GIA, Chicago).

Co-opting God for the cause

The presence of Christians at the assault on the US Capitol building last week appalled me, but it did not surprise me.

Five years ago, I had dinner with the family of a Lutheran priest in America. It was the week in which the news media were constantly replaying a tape of Donald Trump boasting about how he groped women. The oldest daughter, a girl of 12, had asked her mother how a man like that could ever be elected as president. 'What did you say?' I enquired, and the mother replied, 'I didn't say anything. Because if I had told her what I thought, she might have repeated it to some of her school friends, who might then repeat it to their parents, and we could end up losing church members.'

To talk about political issues – whether in connection with race, climate change, women's rights or arms control – is taboo in some American Christian circles. It is regarded as divisive. A clear distinction is drawn between the church and the state … as if race, the environment and world peace were not God's business.

So, on the basis of where Democrats or Republicans stand on abortion, gay rights, black lives or drilling for oil, some people of faith find it easier to choose to stand behind a partisan banner than to openly discuss the ethical and spiritual dimensions of issues of public concern. And when, as witnessed last week, your favoured candidate who has been the defender of your deeply held prejudice is rejected, the unthinking mind regards it as an onslaught against God. And there is no option but for Christian soldiers to fight the good fight.

My experience of such believers – both extreme right and left wing – persuades me that their reading of the Bible is often highly selective, and that they are influenced more by the rhetoric of populist preachers than by any fidelity to scripture. Some, if asked about the social justice injunctions of the Hebrew prophets, might dismiss them as being 'before Jesus'. The same, if asked about Jesus' concern for women, the environment, race or money, would probably say, 'Next question.'

For many other Christians, Trump has been a bogus Messiah. His photo shoot holding a Bible outside a church during a Black Lives Matter protest was not, in my view, an endorsement of faith but an attempt to convince the faithful he was on their side. His ability to stand on a podium, manipulate emotions, pontificate and defy contradiction is in complete contrast to the great religious leaders. They, like Jesus, sat at ground level even among those who disagreed with them to discuss the thorny issues, make themselves vulnerable and affirm the humanity of all.

Thought for the Day
11 January 2021

Legislating for goodness

If you were a woman who had known unwanted interference by men, and who had friends who had been raped, and there was an opportunity to stand in solidarity with other women at a vigil called because of the murder of a woman in your vicinity, what would you do?

If you were a police officer charged with keeping the law and protecting the public, particularly as regards the virulence of the pandemic, and you were asked to attend an illegal vigil at which people were at risk of spreading the virus but refused to disperse, what would you do?

Few people who saw pictures of women being manhandled by police officers on Saturday night at Clapham Common can have been unaffected. Most people will have reacted viscerally, with revulsion.

On the one hand we have women who felt it was right to attend a vigil, and on the other police who believed it was right to uphold the law. Two wrongs may not make a right, but here two rights clearly made a wrong.

It is understandable that in the heat of the moment some might demand a change in leadership of the Met and many more demand tighter laws prohibiting the molestation of women. I would love if there were some story in the Bible which pointed to a solution. But there is no such story – I've scanned the pages.

What there is, however, is evidence that Jesus occasionally broke laws which prohibited the exercising of compassion; and the insight of St Paul, that all the laws in the world cannot legislate for goodness. I want to say that again: all the laws in the world cannot legislate for goodness.

We're dealing here in Britain with what is a universal malady, namely the fact that men (and I know it's not all men) have a propensity to use violence against women. Moreover, when they do so, women are somehow expected to be forbearing and even to take the blame.

Recently we've come to realise that legislation alone will not halt climate change; it requires us to consciously analyse our behaviour, question our assumptions and recognise that the progress we want to see won't just come about through legislation, but also from the deliberate changes we make to the way we live.

Nothing less – nothing less – is required of men in relation to how we treat women.

Thought for the Day
15 March 2021

What shall we tell the children?

In 2013 I gave a seminar at Greenbelt Festival entitled 'Reading the Bible can be bad for your faith'.

It was not a cynical take on the word of God. It was an attempt to highlight two things:

a) That the Bible has been and can be used as a manipulative tool by the power-hungry. In this context I looked at its use by the supporters of apartheid in South Africa. I could equally have alluded to religious misogyny.

b) Secondly I wanted to suggest that when we open the Bible, we are dealing with an assortment of literatures which deserve different but appropriate kinds of engagement. We don't read a poem in the same way as we read a letter. We don't read a textbook in the same way as we read a biography. The different literary genres of the Bible therefore have to be respected.

I illustrated this by looking at the stories which we may call historically true and others which tell a truth about God and humanity. The Exodus from Egypt is history, but the story of the prodigal son is not. It's a parable.

Afterwards I was approached by a boy and his mother. He was rather bemused at the distinction I had made between a true story and a truth story. Did that mean that I was doubting the Bible as the inerrant word of God? The next day a man who had been at the seminar with his 12-year-old son similarly alluded to a puzzling conversation he had had with the boy on their drive back home.

I felt no need to defend what I said. I stand by it completely. But I did feel that, in loyalty to these two boys, it is perhaps appropriate to consider what we tell children about God and faith and the Bible.

The difficult stage

Now, from a psychological perspective it would be fair to say that when a young person is going through puberty and early adolescence, the changes in their physical, emotional and sexual systems produce enough confusion as they gradually try to embrace the person they are becoming without their religious foundations being shaken.

I can vividly remember at the age of 13 ironing my clothes because my mother said it was time I took on that responsibility for myself. Into the house one evening came our next door neighbour as I was doing due diligence to my shirts. She noticed that I was unusually silent (sullen even) and said to my mother, 'Your John's not saying much, Mrs Bell.' To which my mother replied, 'No. He's at the difficult stage.' Internally I wanted to scream, 'No, I'm not at the difficult stage. It's my mother who's at the difficult stage.'

If at this age, when so much is in turmoil, someone suggests to an adolescent believer that the Bible deserves to be read in more than a purely literal way, this might not be what they either want or need to hear. To some, such a suggestion might constitute a threat to what they regard as unassailable faith, an anchor to hold on to when all else is drifting. To others such a suggestion might be a liberation.

So what do we tell the children?

Instruction is not all

Let me begin by almost undermining the title by saying that telling things to children is not the only – and sometimes not the best – conduit to faith.

The Roman Catholic church uses a term which Protestants don't seem to favour. It is *liturgical formation*. It refers to how what we do repeatedly as regards private prayer and engagement in communal worship helps to form faith as much as what we are told about God. What we do repeatedly, and what we see those we love doing repeatedly, can have a profound subliminal impact.

I have spoken to and read about innumerable people for whom the humble piety of their parents established their belief in God. Here are two examples:

1) A Dutch friend called Jaap had a father who always read his children Bible stories with the same fervour, animation and affection as he would read a bedtime story. And he chose not just the tender words of Jesus and the comforting psalms. He read them stories from the book of Judges about a woman who put a tent peg through a man's skull. And about a left-handed swordsman who put his sword through a fat king's belly. And about how on one occasion a crowd of cheeky boys made a fool of Elisha the prophet because he was baldy.

   My friend's affection for scripture is rooted in the storytelling of his father.

2) Marie was a Roman Catholic girl whose father worked in a factory. She remembers with great fondness how every night he came home, tired from work, and would hang up his coat and hat in the hall. Then he came into the living room, and before he conversed with the family, he'd kneel down before a small shrine in the corner of the room, bless himself and pray silently for a few moments.

   Marie's faith is rooted in that repeated act of reverence which was so dear to her father.

Before the age of literacy, what we ingest from other people can stay with us for good. And some of that will also come from what we sing and the way we engage with scripture.

Three songs

My theology has been shaped by three songs I learned before I could read.

The first was taught me by Ina Carey, a beautiful woman who was my first Sunday School teacher when I was around three years of age.

There was an older girl in our church whom I'll call Maureen Andrews. She had the singular ability to be sick in Sunday School. We would be playing at Daniel in the lion's den or colouring in Solomon's palace and we would hear *Whrrruugh* ... and big Maureen would deposit her breakfast on the floor.

Miss Carey would quickly take Maureen out to get fresh air, and return with a brush, shovel and sawdust to wipe up the mess. That done, she would return smiling to the front of the class and sing:

Praise him, praise him, all you little children;
God is love, God is love.

I used to think: If God is anything like Miss Carey, able to clean up big Maureen's boke (Scottish for vomit) and then to smile and sing, God must be marvellous. My first picture of God was not as an old man or a judge or someone sitting on a cloud. God was love. And because Ina Carey so well represented that love of God, I never found it difficult to believe that God is not an alpha male.

My mother taught me another song:

Jesus loves me

... and this in a primitive way convinced me that the beautiful love which was in God had been intended for wee John Bell aged three, and that Jesus had come to tell me that.

And my very practical grandmother taught me this song:

Oh what can little hands do
to please the king of heaven?
The little hands some work may try
to help the poor in misery.
Such grace to mine be given.

Thus I learned that if God was love and Jesus came to show me that love, then my response had to be to share God's love in acts of kindness and justice.

All my theology is based on these three songs ... which I remember because I learned them before I could read, and they will be with me until I die, and be inside me even should I end up with Alzheimer's. It leads me to ask what are the truths we enable children to ingest which will stay with them for ever. I don't want to be disparaging of light-hearted songs which children of course should sing. But what kind of lasting spiritual succour will they receive if every Sunday School song is of the entertainment variety, such as:

I have curly wurly hair.
Mine is brown but yours is fair.
God made your hair and eyeballs too
and did the same for the kangaroo.

A song such as this from Bernadette Farrell would be much more helpful:

God made me as I am,
part of creation's plan.
No one else can ever be
the part of God's plan that's me. [1]

What we do with kids

Recently I was working in a deprived neighbourhood in the Midlands where there is a very valiant church with a lovely Anglican priest. Each year at Christmas and Easter classes from the primary school come to church, and the congregation helps to make that a special day. They don't just have a school service, they decorate the church and detail specific places where different people will tell one part of the story of Christmas or of the passion, death and resurrection of Jesus. Children walk round as if on a mini pilgrimage.

Two years ago, during the Holy Week visit, the priest heard some children talking as they were making their way to church. One boy, who was repeating a year, had been at the seasonal events before. He told his friends, 'I know what's going to happen. They're going to tell us about how the baby Jesus got crucified.'

One of the things which became apparent to the priest was that as good as it was for the church to celebrate the two major feasts with children, it can give a very impoverished perspective on Jesus. If these are the only episodes in his life about which children are told, they are being introduced to a very passive Jesus. He lies in his mother's arms and he hangs on the cross. There must be more.

And there is.

More recently I was in another deprived neighbourhood, this time in Yorkshire. The local church also has regular visits from schoolchildren. But it is not twice a year. It is once a week for a couple of months, and it is for all kids in primary two.

The church has a room which is designated solely for Godly Play – a method of engaging children physically and imaginatively with Bible stories. As well as activities with objects, the children are encouraged to get inside the story, to wonder at it, to work out which person they most relate to. It is not coercive evangelism, it is creative engagement.

It used to be that year two would come for eight weeks. Then the head teacher asked if they could come every week because it brought immense benefits to the rest of the children's education in class ... opened them to wonder, to questions, to discovery.

Neither the songs nor the activities are about instruction. Rather they are means by which the children appropriate for themselves the truths about God and the stories in scripture.

Sowah Mensah

I divert for a moment to recount an incident which fascinates me every time I repeat it. It comes from Sowah Mensah, a drummer from Kenya who occasionally works in the USA.

He speaks of how in his country there was a tribe whose history had never been written down. An American university heard of this and before long there was an agreement that staff and post-graduate students from the anthropology department would come over and transcribe their oral history. In due course researchers interviewed many of the tribespeople, asking them about famous names, battles, and plagues which affected the tribe; they recorded their wisdom sayings and some of their songs.

All the data was sent back to the university in America where it was analysed. The researchers were amazed at how most accounts harmonised with each other. The interviewees had remembered things in a similar chronological order.

In time the history was published, and the professor in charge of the project came to present the book to the people. There was ceremony and ritual after which the professor thanked the tribe for the rare privilege given to his department, and handed the book over to the tribal chief. The chief thanked the professor, then walked into his tribe with the book, opened it and tore out the pages, handing one to each person who, in turn, ate the page.

Understandably the professor was a bit puzzled by this response, so at an appropriate time he asked the chief, 'Why, when I gave you the book, did you tear it up; and why did the people eat the pages?'

To this the chief replied, 'Because if this is our story, it should be inside us.'

The Bible is our story

The Bible is our story, and it should be inside us ... not because we are told what to believe about it, but because only if it is within and not on the page can it nourish us. And it will be the songs we sing, the way we read it to children, the activities that enable it to be embodied which will allow trust in it and faith to grow from it.

We should not be sidetracked into thinking that intellectual understanding at an appropriate age is the only way. I did not first engage with Charles Dickens by reading literary criticism. I began with reading an abridged version of David Copperfield. Then when I studied English my appreciation became deeper, only because I began with the story and not the interpretation.

How I love a song I heard in a Mennonite church in Winnipeg. It was sung by adults and children a dozen times each Sunday before the Bible was read:

> Listen to the Word which God has spoken,
> listen to the One who is close at hand.
> Listen to the voice behind creation,
> listen even if you don't understand.

Now given that not everything can be conveyed through songs and activity, what might be some of the salient truths we would want children to ingest as much from experience as from formal learning? I am not going to give a prescriptive list; I am merely pointing up some aspects of belief which are biblically verifiable and which may be pertinent to the world of today and tomorrow.

On reading the Bible

With regard to the Bible, I think we should stop calling it a book which children have to read and begin to call it God's Family Album with which they engage themselves.

Too often the Bible is offered as if what it contains is primarily about behaviour. But Gospel is not law or moralism, nor are the Psalms, the history books or the prophets. We need to widen the scope.

I go for *family album* because it has snapshots of God and the people of God.

In the Bible, God metaphorically-speaking keeps changing his clothes – sometimes a wrestler, or a laughter-maker, or a midwife, other times a judge, an architect or even the sound of silence. We see God in different guises, just as in a collection of photographs of our family we see our spouses, parents, children and acquaintances continually dressed in different garb. It all depends on what they were doing and where they were. Mothers are not always mothering, children are not always behaving.

God's people are also in the family album – the very wonderful and the very weird. They are seen together as pilgrims, as an army, as a nation, as a persecuted community. And among them some individuals are singled out for a special profile – because of their virtue or their vices, through a record of their actions, or because of letters they have written or criticisms of society they have made.

There are some very boring parts … just as when you come across the guest list for your grandparents' wedding and wonder, 'Who were all these people?' There are some saucy bits which give odd descriptions of the female anatomy: 'My beloved has breasts like clusters of grapes.' (*Song of Songs 7:7*)

The male does no better: 'My beloved has thighs of alabaster.' (*Song of Songs 5:15*)

There are family proverbs and sayings which have been passed down for centuries. And among these are stories about Jesus and words of Jesus without which we can't make sense of the other things that are written, because he is the head of the family. And it is in the light of his life and teaching that we have to see everything else the Bible contains.

Now, as to salient biblical truths for today?

1) God loves the world

Christian theology and traditional Christian education have detracted from this truth through a myopic reading of John 3:16.

> *God so loved the world*
> *that he gave his only son that whoever believes in him*
> *should not perish but have everlasting life.*

This verse, as flagged up by people who hand out biblical tracts, normally has two distractions associated with it.

The first is that it is frequently accompanied by an illustration of Christ on the cross – this despite it being from John 3 and not 19. The verse does not appear immediately before the crucifixion, it comes directly after Jesus' conversation with Nicodemus. So while it is a salvation text, it is not primarily about Calvary.

The second error is the overlooking of the fifth word.

God so loved …   Jews?
                  Baptists?
                  Tele-evangelists?
                  Members of the General Synod?
                  Stained-glass windows?

God so loved the *world* … and the word for the world in Greek is *cosmos*.

It is an ecological as well as an ecumenical affection which is in the heart of God. It is for the fabric of the universe as well as for the salvation of souls. Indeed, I would go further and argue that one of the results of faith should be a kindling of affection for the world which God made, put into our guardianship and continues to love.

Previous thinking about the world sometimes saw it as a realm which was solely for admiration as in the beloved hymn:

All things bright and beautiful,
all creatures great and small.

Or the world was regarded as an entity in which humanity proved its worth by 'mastering' it. Apart from the fact that this is not a biblical mandate, the ecological crisis which we face should convince us of the folly of trying to master a planet whose systems we even yet do not fully understand despite millennia of human endeavour.

I am suggesting that ecology should be part of our faith witness to those who come after us, for whom also the world was made. Young people, who are increasingly vocal about the toxic legacy they are inheriting through decades of denial about detrimental human activity, should not come at this solely through Greenpeace or Friends of the Earth. If they have anything to do with the Christian faith, they should discover that we worship a God who loves the world, and unless we love it too, our discipleship will be partial, concerned with egocentric humanism and not what God in creation has so generously given us.

As regards the universe, unless we are seven-day creationists, let us be Christian adults who accept the scientific theories of creation as well as the biblical narratives. We should not allow another generation of children to have a crisis of belief because the Bible says that God made the world in seven days and Charles Darwin says something different.

What we are dealing with are different windows onto the truth which are not mutually exclusive. We should be able to speak of religion as the partner of science rather than its enemy.

If I were trying to explain this to teenagers, I would do three things.

a) I would give them a fairly boring paragraph or two to read from a book on family therapy. I'd choose a section which deals with intergenerational difficulties, particularly between young men and their fathers.

b) I would then play a recording of *All You Need Is Love* by Lennon and McCartney.

c) And finally I would tell them the story of the prodigal son.

After that I'd ask them what the connection was.

They are all, in different ways, about love. One charts the specific ways in which it flourishes or breaks down. One celebrates its importance. The third is a parabolic story which shows what is possible. Three different genres of literature. Three different windows onto family life, each with a different purpose.

I would do this because when we deal with creation, there is a fairly convincing narrative about the beginnings of the world and of life which we might call the scientific window. It draws on the theories of Darwin and others and it is constantly being updated.

The scientific window does not appear in the Bible, but two others do. One is the hymn which begins Genesis. A hymn with seven stanzas and a chorus:

God saw what he had made and it was good.
Evening and morning came ... the second day.

This is what we might call the window of wonder. It delights in creation as an intentional gift of God which has total integrity.

And then Genesis 2 opens a third window which has to do with the meaning and purpose of creation. We might call it the parabolic window ... for it holds up a mirror in which we see human nature in its glory and fallibility.

2) *God loves diversity*

Secondly, I want to suggest that children discover that God has a passion for diversity. I say this in the light of an experiment I did with ten doctoral students at McCormick Seminary in Chicago.

They, like me, had become used to the word diversity being used in conjunction with church debates on human sexuality. It used to be that there was straight and gay; now there are endless varieties, such that rather than say I'm male or female as in the past, today a response with regard to gender might be:

'I'm a bipolar, ambidexterous, hirsute, animal-tolerant, lactose-averse, monosyllabic, agoraphobic, regular kind of guy.'

I asked the students to go into groups for an hour and, without looking up the Bible, but rather relying on their memory, come to a measured assessment of whether God liked or disliked diversity.

Their conversation was intense. It wasn't that people were disagreeing with each other. It was because they were tripping over each other with evidence after evidence of God's option for difference.

The seven days of creation each had a different focus. When God made weather it wasn't always the same. When God made flowers they were not all red roses. When God made animals, he made more than dogs and cats.

When Noah set sail in the ark, he was required to preserve the diversity of the animal kingdom. God wanted to keep the differences.

When the builders of the city and tower of Babel were expelled, it was precisely because they wanted everyone to have one language and one culture – no diversity.

God gave ten commandments and not one. The children of Israel were divided into twelve tribes, not kept as a unitary authority. When the songs and prayers we call the Psalms were collected, they covered an incredible array of subject matter, emotional depth, poetic style and intended purpose.

Jesus chooses disciples who have a range of backgrounds, and has equal engagement with women as with men. He consorts with people who range from an officer in royal service to an alleged call girl, and from a pedigreed member of the Jewish local government to a woman whose race is hated by the Jews. He also associates with people from seven nationalities other than his own, and never condemns any of them for not being Jewish believers.

And when we come to Pentecost, God's bias for diversity is endorsed by the variety of languages in which the Gospel is proclaimed, the variety of gifts which the Spirit endows, and the variety of types and locations of the fledgling churches to which both St Paul and St John the Divine bear witness.

For children, difference should never be seen as an impediment, but part of God's design, whether that be a difference in colour, race, language, physical or mental agility or religion.

If we rear children only to love those who are like them, then we go against the declared will of God, and we must ask what we are doing to bring peace and reconciliation to the world. But if we rear children to find novelty and even delight in the way in which others are different from them, then we are engendering benign curiosity which is a much more kindly force than innate suspicion.

And this has great pertinence to the way in which, as Christians, we honour the equality before God of men and women. We should not tell the stories of the male disciples without telling the stories of the female disciples, if for no other reason than that we know very little about half of Jesus male companions. I mean, who could do a two-page essay on James the Less, or Thaddeus, or

Bartholomew, or Nathaniel, or Phillip ... or even Matthew? And let us not read the heroic stories of Moses and David without also reading the equally heroic stories of Shiphrah and Puah, or Abigail, or Esther, or Rizpah ... all of whom God called as women to stand against the injustice of men.

3) Jesus lived

Thirdly I believe we should tell children that Jesus lived ... especially if we go to churches in which part of liturgical formation consists in saying the creed. For in the creed a life is both abbreviated and eliminated in a comma:

> Born of the Virgin Mary (comma)
> suffered under Pontius Pilate.

There can be few figures in history whose life is disposed of so curtly.

Of course there is a reason for the creed omitting Jesus' life and ministry. It is a collection of theological statements which believers affirm. But, as mentioned earlier, the over-emphasis on the birth and death of Jesus leave little room for discipleship. When we invite people – children and adults alike – to follow Jesus, we cannot expect them to follow him into the cradle or onto the cross. The incarnation and the crucifixion are events which belong to Christ and Christ alone.

But the questions for faith to which they point to are:

> For what was he born?
> and
> Why was he crucified?

It is wholly insufficient merely to say he was born to die, or to trot out some glib phrase present in both Victorian hymns and contemporary worship songs about 'from the cradle to the cross'. I am fed up with meeting adults who see Jesus as some kind of religious pansy whose primary attribute was being nice:

> someone who never laughed out loud
> was even tempered, never got angry
> said pleasantries with which all could agree
> maintained religious traditions
> kept good company
> and was nice to babies and old people.

What a wimp! People who live like that don't end up getting crucified.

If you ask the question 'Why was he born?' you have to answer in terms of his being the living expression of God's love who came to reveal the truth of life and God to the world. If you ask the question as to why he was crucified, you have to answer in terms of how what he did, what he said and who he consorted with were so much of a challenge and disappointment that people wanted to get rid of him.

For people who go on Ignatian retreats, one of the frequent shocks is being asked to use their imagination in opening up a passage of scripture ... to be for a moment the woman at the well, or Zaccheus or Mary of Bethany or Matthew, and to meditate deeply on the encounter.

Some discover that Jesus did not speak Elizabethan English; others that Jesus had more words to say than only those recorded in the Gospels. And some discover that in the flesh and blood interaction between Jesus and those he meets, there is a gamut of conflicting emotions, speeds of speech and deep silences.

This is the Jesus to whom we as adults have to bear witness – one who has a life and does more than appear in a cradle and on a cross.

4) Potential more than problems

We need to say a word about what God's primary interest is in people, and it has to be more than a divine obsession with what they do wrong.

I think my most religious period in life was when I was twelve. On a Sunday morning I would go to two Bible classes and the church service. Each of them began with a prayer of confession.

One on occasion in my early teens, I went to the evening service which also began with a prayer of confession. I wondered what these good Christian people were doing between the end of the morning service and 6.30 pm which required them to rake the depths of their souls for things that were wrong. And I wondered what kind of God it was who needed to hear confession made on my behalf four times in less than twelve hours.

It is not healthy for faith to have an image of God as a deity who is primarily interested in what has gone wrong. It seems to me to be out of kilter with the Gospel. I am not denying the need for repentance or the cleansing of the soul that can come with confession and a declaration of forgiveness. God can deal with what we have done wrong ... but can we deal with what might go right? I rarely if ever heard in my early years in the church the notion that God had planted a wealth of potential within me. It seemed more as if my soul were a spiritual junkyard full of things that kept breaking down.

We tend to read a sin-obsessed God into the scriptures, and this despite the fact that on several occasions, associated with the miracles, Jesus takes to task those who believe that physical or psychological distress is intimately connected with personal sin, and at the same time he points to the potential as yet undiscovered in those who have been marginalised because of their affliction.

He tells a crowded synagogue that a woman who has been crippled for 18 years is nothing less than a daughter of Abraham.

He sends a leper to a priest to confirm his fitness to be reintegrated into society.

He forbids a demoniac whom he cured to follow him. He wants him to become an evangelist in his own village.

He tells Peter that he is a rock and affirms his vocation as well as occasionally upbraiding him.

He points Nicodemus to a fuller understanding of faith which will become possible when he breaks out of his legalistic straightjacket.

He lets a woman whom others call a whore know that she has a capacity to love.

And he gives to an alleged adulteress the right to begin a better life.

All the above seem to me to be about affirming and awakening potential much more than forensically focusing on sin, disobedience and folly. Jesus sometimes brings people into the kingdom through the threat of hell, but more often he loves them into it by persuading them they are worthwhile.

Yet when I ask people to talk about how they imagine people in the gospels, like Zaccheus or Matthew, the typical response is of introverted individuals who are so guilt-ridden that to salve their conscience they give away money swindled from poor people.

I don't know where that notion came from, but it's not in the Bible.

Here is the account of Jesus meeting Zaccheus in Luke's Gospel:

Zaccheus climbed a sycamore tree in order to see Jesus. When Jesus came to the place, he looked up and said, 'Zaccheus, come down here quickly; I'm going to come and stay with you today.' Zaccheus climbed down as fast as he could and gladly welcomed Jesus.

There was a murmur of disapproval. 'He has gone in to be the guest of a sinner,' some people said.

> *But Zaccheus stood there and said to the Lord, 'Here and now,*
> *I give half my possessions to charity. And if I have cheated anyone*
> *I will pay him or her four times over.'*
> *Jesus said to him, 'Salvation has come to this house today for*
> *this man too is a son of Abraham; and the Son of Man has come*
> *to seek and to save what is lost.' (Luke 19:1-10)*

I don't hear Zaccheus confessing any sin. He doesn't say 'Because I have swindled people I'll pay them back,' He says ' If ... IF... I have cheated anyone, I'll pay them back four times over.'

Nor do I hear Jesus agreeing with the cynics that this man was a sinner ... do you?

And if you want to argue that he talks about 'saving those who were lost', that could pertain to exclusion from the community. The only people who talk about sin are the crowd.

The purpose of God in Christ is not solely to convince people of their sin. The purpose of God in Christ is also to convince people of their potential. God has made every child adequate and the job of Christian people is to affirm the potential and awaken the goodness in people who don't think they have much.

This is not a mandate for self-adulation. It is an encouragement to let all of God's children discover the gifts they have to offer. And this dawning of awareness to the fulness of life is, as in Zaccheus, as much part of salvation as anything else. It is his newly discovered generosity which Jesus identifies as proof of his salvation, not a confession of all the sins he had committed since childhood.

5) God has a special interest in young people

We tend to think of young problem-free children as of interest to God. We remember how Jesus blessed the children whom mothers brought to him. But we should not allow adolescents and young adults to be eclipsed.

It was, after all, a girl called Miriam who was the go-between for Moses' birth mother and his adoptive mother. She turned out to be a tambourinist who danced for joy at what God could do. It was a girl a bit older called Esther who won a beauty competition and became the king's favourite consort who was responsible for preventing the genocide of the Jews.

It was an adolescent, David, who was able to do what an army of adults couldn't – eliminate the threat of a military giant by forsaking conventional military wisdom.

It was a boy the same age who did what a crowd could not do – transform selfishness into generosity when he gave his lunch to Jesus so that Jesus might get the crowd to feed itself.

It was five young people –

an epileptic boy,
a centurion's servant
the daughter of a synagogue president
a widow's only son
the daughter of a Syrian woman –

whom Jesus healed and, in the case of Jairus's daughter, put to silence those who claimed that there was no hope for her.

And then there's that lovely story of what happened in the Temple the day after Jesus rode into Jerusalem.

We remember the overturning of the tables. We might just remember him welcoming the blind, crippled and lame people who were normally excluded. But we might not remember the young people, the gang of boys who were shouting the words which their parents had shouted the day before: Hosanna to the son of David. What seemed to have most annoyed the temple clergy was not so much the coarse-throated shouting, but the fact that Jesus was enjoying it.

Remember how he responds to the priestly disdain, and think

of how he said it.

To those, some of whom knew the Psalms by heart, he says:

'... Is there not a verse in the Bible ...?
... Is it maybe in Psalm 7 or is it 8 ...?
Yes I'm sure it's 8 and it will be verse 2 ...
You'll know the line I'm thinking about, gentlemen:

> *God has made his praise sound aloud*
> *out of the mouths of children and babies at the breast.'*

You can just imagine how every time Psalm 8 was recited in the Temple liturgy the priests would seethe with the memory of how Jesus had humiliated them in the face of mere adolescents. And every time these boys heard Psalm 8 being read they would remember the day when Jesus stuck up for them ... as he does for all young people.

Talk delivered at Greenbelt Festival 2014

[1] Copyright Bernadette Farrell 1995, OCP, Portland, OR.

Viva Caledonia

What makes for national identity is a fascinating interplay of mysterious relationships.

And different nations show the predominance of one relationship over all others. So, for example, Australian aboriginal people have been undeniably shaped by their relationship with the natural environment – something which has less significance for urban dwellers.

Affinity to a strong political and philosophical perspective is a primary feature in the identity of a country such as North Korea. Elsewhere a primary feature might be the relationship between the people and the dominant religion – Catholicism in Brazil, Lutheranism in Sweden, Calvinism in Scotland.

Scotland ... that is where I want to end up, because it seems to me that the debate about whether Scotland should be independent of, or integrated within, the United Kingdom is about more than a nationalist or a unionist agenda.

I have grown up in a nation where the interplay between land and history and politics and religion has been and still is a constant. A country which is surrounded on three and a half sides by water with no one living more than 50 miles from the sea makes one aware of physical limitations and of a bigger world beyond. A history which witnesses more to political and cultural subjugation than glorious liberty affects both personal and national self-confidence. A religious culture which – for all its petty censoriousness – has prized the public good of education, philanthropy and social welfare has produced a people who are more sensitive than others to the excesses of unfettered capitalism.

I sometimes wonder what people of my age in the south-east of England would have felt if their school history books had been written in Aberdeen. Or if their accent, religion and culture were regarded as the stuff of comedy. Or if the area which they consider their heartland was spoken of as if it were a far-flung outpost of the Empire.

So when the opportunity comes to consider the future of Scotland, the primary issue is not whether there should be one or two options on a voting slip. We are dealing with something much more mysterious. I would even say holy. We are dealing with the dawning of a liberated self-consciousness. We are dealing with how a people can best fulfil their potential to prosper according to their own lights, to live peaceably with others and to be responsible stewards of the earth. And that – from a biblical perspective – can only happen when a distinct people in their distinct land are free to determine their own future.

We are dealing with a very different heavenly charter from that which requires guardian angels to sing *Rule Britannia*.

Thought for the Day
18 January 2012

Money, money, money

Having just come back from four weeks in North America, I've been pondering a rare practice which took place in one of the churches I visited. The congregation published, every year, how much individual members contributed in their offerings.

I don't know of many churches in the UK which would be keen to emulate this practice, though it used to happen on these shores at a time when people took seriously the principle of giving a tithe – meaning a tenth of their income – to charitable purposes. Nowadays that kind of financial transparency is avoided rather than encouraged. Billionaire philanthropists don't mind their incomes being mentioned on the Sunday Times Rich List. But for other people the public disclosure of their personal wealth is avoided at all costs. For some it only happens as a penalty, inflicted after evidence is produced of unmerited bonuses or misappropriation of funds.

The allegation of financial impropriety is something which seems continually to beleaguer people in public office – whether in the parliaments of this or other nations, or in less prominent municipal authorities. But it is not limited to those in public office, nor is it something which is primarily endemic in the developing world. This was borne in on me a few years ago when I booked a domestic flight. It cost £35, but the travel agent offered me a receipt for £110. When I queried him about the disparity, he said, 'Many of our business customers ask for this. Just claim it on expenses. Nobody needs to know.'

It's easy to point the finger when someone in the public eye is suspected of financial dishonesty, but the truth is that all of us, in different ways, may find ourselves tempted, if not culpable.

If we once claim more on expenses than we should, or if we once pay in cash what should be paid for by card or cheque to enable VAT to be honoured, then any guilt which ensues is more likely to encourage us to do the same again rather than to desist. For, if we are not found out, who needs to know? Why should we need to confess to it? ... and in any case, who would grant us absolution? It's money not morality.

The more I ponder this, the more I am convinced that money is one of the biggest spiritual issues of our day. It can be used – through generosity – to do immeasurable good. But it can also open the door to avarice which, like jealousy, has an all-consuming power and no end of dehumanising effects. No wonder Jesus said you cannot serve God and money. For to believers and non-believers alike, money can, when unaccountable, easily assume the mantle of divinity.

Thought for the Day
7 April 2014

Rampant male heterosexism

The problem-makers

When, in the past, race relations have been at a low point, some-times the phrase 'the black problem' has been used to describe the malaise. This was true of the followers of Eugene Terreblanche and his apartheid-loving backwoodsmen in South Africa, and of right-wing extremists in the USA who were presumed to have the endorsement if not the patronage of President Trump. And it has been behind discriminatory practices regarding BAME commu-nities by national and civic authorities in the United Kingdom. With hindsight, we are able to recognise that the problem is actually with white males who bristle when their presumed superiority is challenged.

When, in the church, the government, or the world of industry and economics, females began to demand equal treatment, the plea was referred to as the 'women's problem'. But, in truth, the problem was men who were culturally conditioned to being in charge and who suddenly feared a loss of profile and privilege.

As regards the 'gay problem', the main protagonists have often been rampant male heterosexuals who – among other things – naively associate male homosexuality with effeminate behaviour, and thereby with women, the idea of whose liberation still causes discomfort.

The biblical view of marriage

On the day I began to write this talk, I heard the news on the radio of how the Anglican Archbishop of Uganda had stated that he would not share communion with those who supported an 'unbib-lical' view of marriage.

Now what exactly is a 'biblical view of marriage'? It could be polygamy, because very few of the Jewish patriarchs stuck to one wife. Abraham had two plus a concubine. His grandson Jacob had two plus two concubines. Samson nearly had a wife, but she married his best man, so he ended up with a prostitute and a devious hairdresser in compensation.

David – the great forebear of Jesus – had as many wives and lovers as he had fingers. And his son Solomon had seven hundred wives and three hundred concubines ... in all of which cases the women were little more than chattels.

Does the Archbishop of Uganda espouse these patriarchal antecedents or would he favour the understanding of marriage approved by St Paul, who states that one reason for getting wed is a lack of self-control? (*1 Cor 7:9*) Paul also spends more time and ink on what he regards as aberrant behaviour in women with respect to headgear, speaking in church and gossip than he does on peculiarly aberrant male traits. And, believing that the world was shortly coming to an end, he comments on how he wishes that others could be like himself – unmarried.

Of course, what the Archbishop was ostensibly criticising was same-sex marriage, which is certainly not mentioned in the Bible. However, most people who have studied the Scriptures would concur that – as regards heterosexual, never mind homosexual, marriage – the Bible is an unlikely sourcebook of helpful hints for fulfilling matrimony.

Lizzie Lowe

I have seldom spoken as openly about homosexuality as I do here, and would have felt no compulsion to return to the subject again, except for what I heard from Nick Burden about Lizzie Lowe.

Nick is the rector of St James and Emmanuel Church in

Didsbury, south of Manchester. It is an evangelical Anglican parish with which I have had fond associations. Earlier this year I heard a radio interview in which he spoke of this girl. Lizzie was an intelligent teenager in the congregation, who occasionally babysat for the vicar and his wife. She had a history of mild depression, but nothing too concerning. Then, one day in 2014 , she took her life. At the coroner's inquest into her death, it was revealed that shortly before it happened she had sent a text message to a friend which said,

'I don't believe that God can love me the way I am.'

She knew herself to be lesbian, but was also aware of the negativity which surrounded any talk of same-sex relationships within her wing of the church. After her death, Nick felt that it was time that the congregation began to think about how it dealt with gay and lesbian people. At the mere mention of such a possible discussion a number of members left.

An isolated incident? I thought so, until two months after hearing of Lizzie, I met a man in a Baptist church who told me that his son had taken his life for exactly the same reason – being perceived as abnormal if not sinful by his faith community.

When recounting both these incidents to a friend of mine, he said that for three or four years suicide was on his own horizon when he realised how abhorrent his sexuality was to the Christians who surrounded him. He only began to gain self-confidence after he had an appointment with someone who specialised in 'deliverance ministry', which aims to turn gay people straight ... except that my friend didn't become straight. The deliverance minister tried to seduce him, and that traumatic episode let him see how much talk of 'deliverance' was a guilt-inducing sham.

Fidelity to Scripture

For many Christian people, and especially for dominant male heterosexuals like the Archbishop of Uganda, the primary issue is about fidelity to Scripture.

A wide view

Taking first of all a wide view, one might suggest that Scripture doesn't have much to say about homosexuality. Conservative and liberal scholars agree that there are five basic texts, two in the Old Testament book of Leviticus, three in New Testament epistles. None of the texts run to any more than three verses. Yet on this limited biblical literature, it is claimed that the credibility of the Bible and Christianity hangs. Some churches, such as an Anglican congregation I visited in Vancouver, have seen lawsuits costing hundreds of thousands of dollars as the 'true Bible believers' separate themselves from fellow members who do not share their opinion and then, on the basis that they are *the* true believers, claim ownership of the church buildings ... all this predicated on five short, unconnected biblical texts.

Why is it that same-sex relationship is spoken of as the dividing line, the point of no return, the litmus test as regards authentic discipleship? Why not divorce, about which not just the Law, but the Prophets, Paul and Jesus have much to say, and nothing very positive? Could it be that a more lenient attitude to divorce favours rampant male heterosexuals ... who might one day want to offload an unwanted wife and children?

Or why not child abuse, about which Christians are remarkably silent, apart from talking up preventative measures? Could it be that child abuse is so unspeakably all-pervasive, which means it happens even within Christian families and Christian churches, and is mainly indulged in by heterosexual men?

These issues would – in terms of personal morality – be much more rational choices for the litmus test of discipleship, given that people choose to get divorced, or knowingly decide to abuse a child. But people like Lizzie Lowe didn't choose to be gay or lesbian. Indeed, who would choose to have a lifestyle of same-sex attraction knowing that in most societies for centuries, if not millennia, the mere whiff of such could bring disapproval, isolation, beatings, imprisonment and even death?

BIBLICAL PERSPECTIVES

Genesis

Because the five 'key' texts, which I will shortly allude to, are becoming ever more suspect in their application, some people go back to the beginning of the Bible, to chapter one of Genesis, a passage commonly regarded as a great poem about God's creative genius. The poem says, 'God made male and female in his image' and told them to 'be fruitful and multiply'. This, in the minds of some, indicates the compulsory biological norm for everyone.

When godly people read the poem we call Psalm 23, 'The Lord is my Shepherd', do they immediately go down on all fours and start bleating like sheep? If not, then why take the poem of creation as literally as if it were a medical prescription?

Or think of chapter two of Genesis, the story of Adam and Eve, which most Christians do not look on as biographical in the same way as they would regard the stories of Abraham and Sarah. In this chapter we read that 'A man leaves his father and mother and clings to his wife and they become one flesh'. *(Gen 2:24)* Amazingly a number of people give that beautiful image, which comes from a *parabolic* story, the status of a sexual commandment indicating that genital copulation is only permissible between people of the opposite sex.

When godly people hear the parabolic story of the Wise and Foolish Virgins, do they immediately look to see if their lamps are full of oil? If we don't normally take poems and parables as literal injunctions from God, why do so with the first two chapters of Genesis?

Added to which, if men and women are exclusively created for procreative marital relations, what does that say about people who are infertile and cannot conceive? What does that say about heterosexual people (of whom Jesus and Paul are two) who don't marry? Are they failing to fulfil the divine mandate to go forth and multiply?

Now let me deal more particularly with ...

The five disputed texts

In preparation for this paper, I decided to read the most thoroughly conservative book on the issue. It has high accolades from a range of academics for its scholarship. It is called *The Bible and Homosexual Practice* by Robert A.J. Gagnon of Pittsburgh Seminary in the USA. [1]

I found the title a bit intriguing. I can understand that someone who is learning the piano has to practise before giving a performance, and that someone who is going to be a tattoo artist has to practise before he or she puts needle to flesh. But does a blue-eyed person have to practise being blue-eyed? Does a left-handed individual have to practise not being right-handed? Does a homosexual have to practise not being a heterosexual?

Sadly, Professor Gagnon doesn't want to deal with the potential in homosexuals to love, laugh, cry, create, empathise, encourage. He's just interested in their sexual 'practice', and contrasts it with how males anatomically fit perfectly into females like a hand into a glove. He regards the conventional position of face to face heterosexual intercourse as obligatory on humanity. This is a recurrent theme, and he does not spare anyone's blushes in endorsing the fiction that homosexual people are not interested in affection, mutual understanding, companionship. No, no! They just want promiscuous coupling. Here is one of his repeated mantras:

> *Homosexual intercourse constitutes a conscious denial of the complementarity of male and female found not least in the fittedness (anatomical, physiological, and procreative) of the male penis and the female vaginal receptacle.*

Another repeated hallmark of this 480-page book is the footnotes – more footnotes sometimes than text – which can be adduced as the mark either of a prestigious academic, or of a haunted obsessive.

Texts in the Hebrew Scriptures

Let me briefly deal with the texts in the Hebrew Scriptures:

> Leviticus 18:22 – *You shall not lie with a male as with a woman. It is an abomination.*

> Leviticus 20:13 – *If a man lies with a male as with a woman, both of them have committed an abomination; they shall be put to death.*

These injunctions come from a legal code much of which is otherwise disregarded by Christians. There is legislation in Leviticus which states that women who are menstruating make anything or anyone they touch unclean. *(Lev 18:19)* Later in the Pentateuch there is a law which prohibits people who are disfigured from entering the place of worship. *(Deut 23:1)* The same book suggests that if a virgin is raped in a town and her cries are not heard, she should thereby be understood to be complicit. *(Deut 22:24)*

Is anyone going to foist *these* ordinances as obligatory on 21st-century believers? Other 'abominations' listed in the law of Moses include persecuting the poor, extortion and idolatry. Why, I beg to ask, is no one making a fuss about these aberrations? ... especially in our present society where the poor are persecuted, innocents are the victims of extortion, and commercialism has made idolatry a new sport.

Pauline texts

The first New Testament text is found in Romans 1:26-27. It appears in a passage in which Paul is speaking about the consequences of idolatry. He says that ...

> *God gave them up to their degrading passions.*
> *Women exchanged natural intercourse for unnatural,*
> *and in the same way also the men,*
> *giving up natural intercourse with women*
> *were consumed with passion for one another.*
> *Men committed shameless acts with men*
> *and received in their own persons*
> *the due penalty for their error.*
> (NRSV version)

Later in 1st Corinthians 6:9 he writes:

> *Fornicators, idolaters, adulterers, male prostitutes, sodomites etc*
> *... will not inherit the kingdom of God.*
> (NRSV version)

And in 1 Timothy 1:10, Paul puts fornicators and sodomites in the same bracket of lawbreaker as slave traders, liars, perjurers and those who murder their parents.

Now, I am not going to dismiss these texts as irrelevant, but I'd like to make a couple of observations.

1) Certain of these 'Pauline' references clearly refer to men who offer same-sex services as well as the committing of *unnatural* acts between people of the same sex.

I want to suggest that these are closely connected, because rampant male heterosexuals don't necessarily keep within their 'natural' sphere of engagement if females are not available. And this is not just an ancient Greek thing.

Until quite recently, in the predominantly Roman Catholic nations of continental Europe, men who felt their erotic impulses unrequited sometimes resorted to having sex with other men. It could have been because their wives were menstruating, or coming towards the end of a pregnancy, or didn't want to have another child. For their rampant heterosexual husbands there was a choice:

a) abstain
b) use another woman ... but that would be adultery
c) use a prostitute ... but that would be a mortal sin
d) use contraception ... but that needed two willing partners and the church forbade it
e) have sex with a man ... not romantic sex, but something which provided release

If that is what Paul was inveighing against when he talked about how men should not give up their natural passions for unnatural, I would applaud him.

2) But supposing your 'natural' passion is not heterosexual? Supposing you have no desire at all to sexually engage with someone of the opposite sex? Supposing the mere thought of it repels you, as much as a heterosexual person is repelled at the thought of indulging in homosexual activity? If God does not want people to engage in unnatural acts, then we have to

look at Paul again, and not consider that *natural* is determined by the majority inclination.

But in addition to this, we have to admit that neither in Leviticus nor in the letters of Paul is there any suggestion that same-sex attraction could be anything other than genital coupling. But read the poets – like George Herbert or Wilfrid Owen or Walt Whitman or Robert Frost, all of them gay – and then ask whether the homosexuality to which they allude is of the same order as bestiality.

Associated texts

The dear Professor Gagnon, in an attempt to buttress his opinions, revisits certain stories in the Hebrew scriptures which have long since been discredited as either 'gay' or 'anti-gay' texts. Some of his conclusions are quite alarming.

The sin of Ham (Genesis 9:18-27)

For example, he regards the sin of Ham as being gay sex.

Ham is one of the sons of Noah who find his father naked and drunk. He goes to call his brothers. They cover up their father, and Noah then curses Ham and his progeny for seeing him in an embarrassing state. Professor Gagnon suggests that Ham had indulged in anal intercourse with his father.

Poor Ham! He has had a bad time of it in recent church history. Fifty years ago, South African pastors in the Dutch Reformed Church were interested in the same passage. But, for whatever reason, they didn't conclude that the sin of Ham was intercourse with his old man; they believed that the reason he was cursed was because he was black.

The sin of Sodom (Genesis 19:1-11)

Then there's the story of Sodom – of how two angels turned up at Lot's door one night, and before long a crowd of men were battering away at it because they wanted to have sex with the angels. I'm not a linguist, but I think there might be an element of naivety in some scholars. There is a four-letter word (which I am not going to repeat) which can mean 'to have intercourse'. But it can also mean to beat up, pulverise, abuse. Maybe that's what the men wanted to do.

Whatever the truth of the terminology, the vast majority of people see, as Jesus did, that the sin of Sodom is a failure to offer hospitality. *(Matt 10:15)* How could anyone applaud this story as a straightforward anti-gay narrative when it includes an episode in which Lot, allegedly a man of God, thought that he could dissuade the men from their sexual or violent intentions by offering them his daughters as substitute angels?

The truth about David and Jonathan (Genesis 18-20)

Professor Gagnon also revisits the relationship between David and Jonathan. I would certainly not claim that this story provides convincing proof of a gay relationship in the Bible. But undoubtedly these men have a deep emotional fondness for each other.

'Not at all!' protests Professor Gagnon. Their relationship is purely political. When Jonathan gives David his armour it is not a sign of affection, it is a sign that he wants him to be the next king. But David was already aware that this was his destiny. He had been anointed for the purpose by Samuel.

As to how their love 'surpassed that of women', Professor Gagnon surmises:

'Jonathan's repeated display of [brackets] *non sexual* [close

brackets] *kindness surpassed anything David had ever known
from a committed erotic relationship with a woman.*'

I presume from this that Professor Gagnon must have access to
reserved information in David's private diary of erotic satisfaction.
I have never read anywhere in the Bible of how much or how little
David enjoyed physical intimacy with any of his several wives.

An alternative perspective on the story

But let a non-prejudiced reader consider that story, and he or she
would find very different resonances.

He or she would perhaps ponder whether Saul was jealous of
the friendship of his son with David. Perhaps he even suspected
it was deeper than a political tryst. Hence he curses Jonathan's
mother ... for making her son not the man he wanted him to be.
Maybe it's a touch of that old message on toilet walls:

A: *My mother made me a homosexual.*
B: *If I give her the wool, will she make me one as well?*

Gagnon also claims that their relationship could never be gay
because sex is never mentioned. Well, in the accounts of David
and his women, the only time sex *is* mentioned is in his adulterous
relationship with Bathsheba. Should the silence of any mention
of sex in relation to his other wives lead us to presume that he
never had sex with them?

I am not claiming the story of David and Jonathan is a gay tract.
But I am suggesting that, depending on your standpoint, intuition
and/or experience, different aspects of the story will invoke different resonances of meaning.

Jesus

Professor Gagnon claims that though Jesus gave no dominical word on it, he was most surely opposed to same-sex relationships. His principal reason for saying this is that Jesus saw himself as fulfilling the law; he therefore stood foursquare on Leviticus. That being the case, Jesus presumably was in favour of women caught in the act of adultery being stoned to death.

The professor also has a very interesting take on Mark 9:42-48 which includes these words:

> *If your eye causes you to stumble ... tear it out*
> *if your hand causes you to stumble ... cut it off*
> *if your foot causes you go stumble ... get rid of it.*

He sees the eye as the part of the body which might encourage lust, the hand as the initiator of masturbation. And the foot? Well, sometimes in Hebrew, feet are a euphemism for the genitals.

We can dissect these stories and play biblical ping-pong with texts till the cows come home. The church has been doing it for centuries and the cows are still in the meadow. I do not for a moment want to erase the contentious texts from the Bible. I want them to stay there as a record of where people who love God once were, but – pray God – are no longer. This is not simply because psychiatrists have long since given up regarding same-sex attraction as a mental illness. This is also because we believe that Jesus fulfils the law ... which is not the same as endorsing the legislation inherited from antiquity. Jesus fulfils the law by calling it back to its original purpose of encouraging relationships of love, honesty, justice and fidelity to characterise the way in which we are connected with God, humanity and the physical universe.

Pastoral considerations

Our reading of Scripture has also to be tempered by pastoral considerations. This was true of Jesus. The pastoral situation made him honour rather than condemn the 'immoral' woman who wiped his feet with her tears. *(Lk 7:47)* The pastoral situation made him open to the touch of a woman who was losing blood *(Mk 5:25)* – a circumstance in which the law should have made him determined to repel her. The pastoral situation made him break with time-honoured practice regarding dead bodies when he touched the corpse of the son of the widow of Nain. *(Lk 7:14)* All of these actions of Jesus were at odds, in the eyes of the legalists, with scriptural teaching.

I realised the importance of pastoral claims in my reflections on the death of Lizzie Lowe. Individuals and congregations can have watertight biblical theology, but it was pastoral considerations which often changed Jesus' heart in the face of those who wanted to object, 'But this is what the Bible says!'

Final observations

Now let me make some observations and then a personal comment.

1) Gay Christians are not exclusively from one wing of the church. I suppose I know as many people who are gay and evangelical as I know those who are gay and liberal. Similarly, those who are against same-sex relationships do not belong to one sector of the church's theological spectrum.

2) Many gay Christians of previous generations were in heterosexual marriages for fear of being discovered. Within my denomination, the evangelical counsel offered to men who said that they were gay was often, 'Perhaps you will find an understanding woman.'

I don't know what this says about women, never mind gay men. What was a woman in such a relationship to understand? Was it that the man who at the altar vowed to love and cherish her would have to fake it when it came to sex? This is not an exceptional situation. With little effort, I can remember the names of at least ten male clergy, most of whom are now deceased, who had entered into marriage primarily to avoid suspicion.

3) If gay people have an antipathy towards the church, it may just be because in previous eras, when homosexual men and women were being brutalised and browbeaten, Christians were reticent to intervene.

Curing queers

There was a book published recently by Tommy Dickinson who is a lecturer in Nursing at Manchester University. It is called *Curing Queers* [2] and it provides alarming detail of the way in which in the 20th century gay people were treated in mental hospitals at a time when homosexuality was considered to be a disease.

Before I directly refer to it, it might be interesting to remember that it is only relatively recently that homosexuality has been regarded as an innate state of being.

1948   The Kinsey Report, based on up to 12,000 interviews, suggested that homosexuality was not as rare as presumed.

1954   The Wolfenden Committee was initiated to investigate homosexual persons and the law. They interviewed only three homosexuals, all from the educated middle class.

1957   The Wolfenden Report was published. It recommended more humane treatment for gay people and the decriminalisation of same-gender sex. Nothing moved for 10 years.

1967   The British Parliament decriminalised same-sex activity between consenting adults in England and Wales. The same did not become true for Scotland until 1981, and 1982 for Northern Ireland.

1992   The World Health Organization withdrew homosexuality from its diagnostic manual.

Back to Tommy Dickinson's book, and to the kind of treatment homosexuals were forced to undergo until the 1970s in an attempt to 'cure' them:

In the treatment of sexual deviants two powerful conditioned stimuli were used: chemical and electrical. The electrical aversive technique consisted of giving electric shocks via electrodes fixed to the patient's wrists, calves or feet. Patients would be asked to fantasise as well as watch pictures of men in various states of undress. In some cases electric shocks were associated with erections above a certain size, measured by a plethysmograph (a pressure detector encircling the penis).

Chemical aversion techniques utilised apomorphine, an emetic which produced nausea and vomiting in the patient. When the medication had become effective, the patients were usually shown pictures of undressed men (*after which they would discover themselves wanting to be sick*).

One of the people subjected to electrotherapy offered this reflection: 'I remember the excruciating pain of the initial shock; nothing could have prepared me for it. Tears began running down my face and the nurse said, "What are you crying for? We've only just started!"'

Alan Turing

It is salutory to remember what happened to Alan Turing. This is the man who cracked the Enigma code. He was the victim of police surveillance in 1952 because he was suspected of being gay. He was eventually caught, in his home, in a compromising position and appeared in court, charged with the crime of 'Gross Indecency'. He was given the option of a period of imprisonment or chemical castration. He chose the latter, and committed suicide in 1954.

Since then, over 25 universities worldwide have named departments or lectureships after him, and according to a biography of him by Jack Copeland,

> *It has been estimated that his breaking of the Enigma code shortened the war in Europe by two years and saved over 14 million lives.* [3]

Of course, he was not the only casualty. Before the Second World War, in 1939, the number of men who were prosecuted for sodomy in the UK was 718. In 1955, it was two and a half thousand.

James Anderton – God's copper

And prosecutions continued to rise even after the publication of the Wolfenden Report, without a murmur of disquiet from Christian quarters. Indeed some prominent Christians encouraged malevolent behaviour ... people like God's copper, James Anderton, the Chief Constable of Manchester 1976-1991. He was a devout Christian who encouraged young constables to go to places which gay men patronised, make themselves look seductive and then arrest anyone who showed an interest.

During this same period secular counsellors and psychiatrists alike protested – in the light of detailed research – that so-called *deliverance* ministries could not turn homosexuals into heterosexuals. But people of faith still believed otherwise. Is it any wonder that given this attitudinal history, the churches have lost the respect and even interest of young generations who do not just believe the message that it's OK to be gay, but regard homophobia (not homosexuality) as an offence?

American perspectives

David Myers is Professor of Psychology at Hope College, Michigan. He is a world-renowned scholar and a Calvinist Christian who changed his mind on this subject. From their analyses of the increasing number of irreligious 'nones', researchers Robert Putnam and David Campbell have discerned that homosexuality' is proving to be 'the single strongest factor' in alienating today's youth and young adults from the church. (*As cited in 'More are Straight, Some are Gay and Why it is that Way' in the* Christian Educators Journal *2016.*)

Writer Amy Sullivan has observed that the church's anti-gay public image 'has been devastating for the image of Christianity'.

When the Barna Group polled Americans ages 16 to 29 on what words best describe Christianity, the top response was 'anti-homosexual'.

In more derisive words, here is how some academics explain the declining religiosity of young Americans:

'In states where they have enacted their hard-right agenda, the polls show a huge backlash from Millennials and young people who are much more tolerant of gays, other races, and much more pro-science and feminist in orientation. These young people have not switched to more liberal Christian denominations, but left religion altogether.'
(*http://www.skeptic.com/eskeptic/15-07-01/#feature*)

The clerical bias

When one reflects on the way in which church debates about homosexuality have been reported in recent years, there has been a reprehensible lack of attention to how lay people, including young people, are affected. It seems as if the dominant rhetoric has been about whether priests and ministers can or cannot be gay, can or cannot be in a civil partnership, can or cannot bless a civil partnership or perform a same-sex marriage. The crucial issue is not about what is appropriate for a gay Christian clergyman or woman. The crucial issue is about how God's laity are treated.

I am not dismissing the significance of the concerns of gay clergy. And I applaud within my own country the commitment given, despite the vitriol experienced, by Kelvin Holdsworth, a priest of the Scottish Episcopal Church, and Scott Rennie, a minister in the Church of Scotland.

However when people offer themselves for ordination, they know the church's stance. And they have to decide whether to live with it or fight against it. Most lay people now know the church's stance on what the clergy can or cannot do. But they don't know whether to include or exclude, whether to support or patronise, whether to treat as normal or as 'intrinsically disordered' those gay people who are brave enough to stay in the church. And gay and lesbian people within our churches are in an ambiguous situation. In some denominations they can have a civil partnership blessed. But, to coin an old phrase, 'How far can they go?' Are they permitted or encouraged to live with each other in a state of sexual and emotional fidelity, or are they expected to remain celibate?

To put it more poetically: Are they allowed to smell the cakes but not allowed to eat them?

I am not here to advocate a plan of action – ten things you must do to make gays welcome. But I raise this issue because I do not want the importance of the Gospel to be eclipsed any longer by the continuing prevalence of an anti-gay narrative in churches. And I deeply believe that – to use Jesus' phrase – we should be more concerned with the 'weightier matters of the law' than with spending endless time and rhetoric trying to discern a putative golden thread which allegedly links disconnected texts in the Hebrew and New Testament Scriptures.

But there is also another reason why I have presented this paper.

Personal interest

I have a vested interest in this issue … because I am gay. This is not a confession. It's an admission. You can confess a sin, but you admit the truth. This information may be new to you, but it's not new to me. I have known that as my sexual identity from before I could read. And I wouldn't change it, because I believe that this is how God made me.

I don't have a partner, nor have I ever had for over thirty years since I was told in no uncertain terms by a superintendence committee that I had to choose between my vocation and a relationship. I have never intentionally admitted this about myself in public before, for a number of reasons:

My denomination gave me important work to do. I was the convener of its liturgical committee, after which I was in charge of the preparation of a new denominational hymn book, and I did not want these jeopardised by what might have been a diversionary interest in my sexuality.

I work as a team with three other people. We share the same salary pool. We have to make our own money and I did not want our work to be compromised if people decided against employing us because one of us was gay.

I have always believed that if the truth is true, it should not be dependent on someone with a vested interest declaring it. Aware that I have a minor public profile I did not want people to be more compassionate towards gay people just because I was one. And so I have tried to encourage both rampant masculine heterosexuals and more moderate male friends to take a positive stand regarding gay people. And several have done that – sometimes to their cost.

But these considerations alone would not have brought me to self-disclosure. It was the suicide of Lizzie Lowe which convinced me that as long as there are still young people who doubt that God loves them on account of their sexuality, then those of us who are not constrained by our work, who are gay and who know the love of God should not keep silent.

Talk delivered at Greenbelt Festival 2017

[1] *The Bible and Homosexual Practice* by Robert Gagnon (Abingdon Press 2001)
[2] *Curing Queers* by Tommy Dickinson (Manchester University Press 2015)
[3] *Turing* by B. Jack Copeland (Oxford University Press 2014)

The omnipresent divide

Years ago, when I was working at a conference in Orlando, Florida, the participants regularly warned each other not to cross the railway line. One day I went against the preferred advice, found the railway line and crossed it. In a few yards I moved from an affluent environment of fun-loving holidaymakers into a ghetto of people who were black, poor, and living in hovels.

Later, when I mentioned to my fellow delegates where I had been, they sat open-mouthed with disbelief that I had ventured there and come back untouched.

That evening, I spoke with one of the hotel staff, a young black man who, I discovered, lived on the other side of the railway line. We had a long conversation about things of which I knew nothing but which were reality for him in Orlando: limited job prospects, the need to own a car to get to work because of poor public transport, a reliance on charities for food and clothing to supplement his low income, a paucity of belief in the possibility of self-improvement.

Here, in a sunspot favoured by many British citizens, were two cities – a neighbourhood stuck in the mire of social deprivation, and a huge tourist village where the lifestyles of the relatively affluent were serviced by people who lived in poverty.

This is not a phenomenon peculiar to the USA. Last year Oxfam indicated that 85 of the world's richest people own the same wealth as 3.5 billion of the poorest; and at this week's World Economic Forum at Davos, the information will be shared that half of all global wealth is owned by 1% of the world's population. Doubtless, people will make the case that this obscene imbalance must be addressed, not only because it's bad for the poor, but also because it's a rot which can threaten the very future of capitalism.

But I'm not sure that convincing arguments are sufficient to turn the tide. I think steps have to be taken to ensure that the privileged come into contact with the poverty of those who create their wealth, so that they may be touched physically and spiritually by the poor.

Failing which, I hope that someone tells the offensive story of the Good Samaritan. For Jesus meant it to be offensive. It's not about a philanthropist with a troubled conscience who offers a handout. It's about a man who crosses the railway line, not to photograph the victim, but to tend to him, accompany him and, having heard his experience, to redistribute his own wealth.

It has always challenged me, that story. Because it exalts personal contact over platitudinous theory. It says, if you're not prepared to be touched by the poor, don't bother to talk about poverty.

Thought for the Day
21 January 2015

The ally of God

I have long suspected the claim that 'music is the international language'. My suspicion was partly fuelled on reading this appalling observation made by the Revd Dr Wauchope Stewart in a lecture about church music given in 1926:

There is a vast difference between the frenzy induced in the savage by the beating of a tom-tom and the peace and solace that steal over the heart as we listen to one of Bach's Organ Chorale Preludes.[1]

Clearly Dr Stewart regarded an appreciation of western baroque music as the litmus test of civilisation. He probably had no understanding of the sophistication of Ghanaian drumming, the complexity of Indian sitar improvisation, or even the artistry involved in playing the bagpipes.

Well, thank God such narrow attitudes have now disappeared … as is evident in the diverse range of music in the current Proms series. Last night there were two great concerts featuring music by native Brazilian composers – classical and jazz – whose rhythms would doubtless have Dr Stewart birling in his grave.

And interested audiences are no longer as homogeneous as they once were. I noticed this last week when, in a street in Amsterdam, I heard Vivaldi's *Four Seasons* consummately played on two violins, an accordion and a bass balalaika, to the adulation of a crowd representing at least thirty nationalities.

Even British churches, whose singing Dr Stewart was keen to pickle in musical formaldehyde, have widened their selection of hymnody to include music from Asia, Africa and the Americas. But naïve or blinkered as the dear doctor may have been, he elsewhere made more profound observations, as when he suggested that there was an intrinsic connection between music and religion, on the basis that unlike other art forms music does not take its substance from the known world.

Most literature, drama, poetry and visual art is based on what has been observed in human life and the physical universe. But not music.

We don't see the first bars of Beethoven's *Fifth* as we might see Picasso's *Guernica*. We cannot hold in our hand and connect with Barber's *Adagio* as we can hold in our hand and read *Harry Potter*. Most of us can't – of our own volition – conjure up the sound of Gershwin's *Rhapsody in Blue*. The music may be in front of us, but it has to be played and experienced to become real.

Music is therefore probably a medium more suited to spiritual reflection than any other art form. It may take us into ourselves, it may take us out of ourselves, and as such may rightly be called the handmaid and ally of God.

Thought for the Day
25 August 2016

[1]   *Music in Church Worship*. Baird Lectures 1926. Pub: Hodder & Stoughton

In favour of a black and feminist Jesus

Roots

It is interesting – if you have a spare moment – to ask yourself what formed your world view, your attitude to faith, your sense of justice. Was it something someone said, was it what you read, was it something you saw?

When I was once asked about the roots of my concern for justice, I found myself strangely moved by something I had long forgotten.

Kilmarnock's shame

It was when I was sixteen and every weekday I would go to my grandparents' house for lunch. They lived only a few hundred yards from my high school.

I loved going there, because – like the best grandparents – they were much better listeners and more interesting talkers than my parents. (At least this was my perspective.) They had lived through two world wars and they could testify from experience what happened to people who were poor or ill before the advent of the welfare state.

One day in 1967, my grandfather let it be known that he was no longer going to support Kilmarnock Football Club. This was startling news. He had supported the team for almost 70 years. I had gone to matches with him. But no longer.

The reason seemed at first to be unconnected. It had to do with the country then known as Rhodesia which the previous year had declared UDI … unilateral independence from Britain. The minority white government wanted to continue to rule the country. Other former British colonies such as Malawi and Zambia had stayed within the Commonwealth but were governed by black African leaders.

The white Rhodesian prime minister, Iain Smith, was unmoved by overtures from the British government to change his mind. In its new independent state it severed links with the UK, but when sanctions and isolation began to bite, it decided that some attempt should be made to keep in with the old country. So the regime decided to send the all-white national football team to Great Britain in the hope of playing with any British clubs which would give them a game. Kilmarnock was one of several which offered themselves. And at that point my grandfather decided to end his support.

He had never been to Rhodesia. He had never met an African. Kilmarnock, with the exception of the Ping Shang Chinese restaurant, was a thoroughbred Ayrshire town. But he – though not a religious man – believed there was something so wrong in racial discrimination that to be neutral in the face of it was not an option.

That was the day when I realised what injustice was and what justice demanded. And it was also the day when I recognised that racism was a reality.

A dormant racist gene?

Indeed, since then I have sometimes wondered whether in all of us there is, if not a racist gene, then certainly a predilection to relate positively or negatively to people we meet on the basis of their racial or national identity. That may come from a bad experience with citizens of another country. You may have been harangued by drunken Russians when sipping a Pimm's on the Costa del Sol; or given a history lesson in Scottish inventors by a drunk Glaswegian on a no. 38 London bus heading to Islington.

Or it may be something you have taken in from the media or books. For example, I used to feel slightly uncomfortable when I met someone from Germany. It was irrational. My family had German friends and I had visited the country. But I remember that, as a child, the war comics I read demonised Germans and Japanese alike. Indeed in the street where I lived we would sometimes play at being British and German soldiers fifteen years after the war had ended.

A white eunuch?

My sense that a dormant, unwitting racist gene is present within us was endorsed by a Bible study in which I was involved two years ago in Florida. At this particular event, a group was reflecting on the story of the Ethiopian eunuch (*Acts 8:26-40*), and in the conversation I became a little bit of a celebrity because I was the only one in the group who could pronounce the word *eunuch* easily.

We hadn't been talking for long when someone asked whether this was the first time in the New Testament that a black person was mentioned. At this an older woman from the Southern States said rather grumpily,

> 'Just because he came from Ethiopia doesn't mean to say that he was black.'

And at this a young black man sitting next to me looked at the woman and said,

> 'Lady, don't take away my colour.'

There was an awkward pause. And I wondered why the woman had raised a doubt about the eunuch's colour, because whenever Ethiopians are mentioned in the Bible there is a presumption they have a dark skin. The leopard can't change his spots, and by extension Ethiopians can't change their blackness.

Indeed if the Ethiopian had been white, it would have been so exceptional that the New Testament – which is gloriously lacking in adjectives – would surely have mentioned it.

Was it perhaps, that coming from the South of the USA, indeed from a state which was reticent to abolish slavery and where white supremacy was still *de rigueur*, she felt that all significant biblical men must be white.

I spoke afterwards to the young black man. His name was Andrew. He had no grievance against the white woman. They went to the same church and later they were happily talking to each other. But I wanted to know whether he perceived white people as carriers of a latent racist gene.

Cone's book

The next day he gave me a book by James Cone, a black theologian recently deceased. It was called *The Cross and the Lynching Tree*.[1]

The book does two things. It records how within Christian communities in the USA the abolition of slavery did not mean the end of discrimination. I think most of us would be aware of that. Had discrimination ended, there would have been no need for God to call out prophetic figures like Malcom X and Martin Luther King. But what I had been blissfully unaware of was the communally approved murder of blacks by whites, even Christian whites, who regarded them as low, filthy and despicable beings.

In the song *Strange Fruit*[2] Billie Holiday, and a succession of black female singers after her, alluded to the public lynchings of black people for no other reason than that their colour was deemed offensive. In small towns in the South, hundreds of people would come to watch an African American who had allegedly offended a white person be tied to a tree, ritually humiliated, sometimes castrated, and then hung.

This happened not in the 1860s after the abolition of slavery in the USA but into the 1960s, and Christians were often in the audience.

Apart from revealing the history and extent of lynching, Cone also offers some theological perspectives on Jesus which are not consonant with those of his white counterparts. Theology like history, as Cone indicates, is usually told from the side of the victors, the successful, the articulate. And so the teaching about Jesus which black people heard from white preachers depicted Jesus as a Caucasian.

Another African-American theologian, Kelly Brown Douglas, in her book *The Black Christ*,[3] cites an anecdote from the life of the late black tennis star Arthur Ashe.

Every Sunday, Arthur Junior went to a church with his parents where he would look up at a picture of Christ with blond hair and blue eyes and wonder if God was on his side.

Howard Thurman who was a respected black theologian of a former generation remembered his grandmother's testimony of how during the days of slavery, the master's minister would occasionally hold services for the slaves. Always the white minister used as his text something from Paul. At least three times a year he would quote:

'*Slaves be obedient to them that are your masters as unto Christ.*'
(Ephesians 6:5)

Regarding this, Thurman's grandmother said,

'*I promised my Maker that if I ever learned to read and if freedom ever came, I would not read that part of the Bible.*'

(It is interesting that the preacher read the word 'slaves' because in the King James Bible, that term is never used. It is 'servants', which sounds more euphemistic. Clearly the plantation preachers were keen to use a different term and probably defended it as 'more in keeping with the Greek'.)

The Caucasian Jesus

For generations of black and indigenous people in the Americas, Jesus was introduced to them by white Westerners as a Caucasian European, often dressed in regal garments befitting of Western courts.

And this white Jesus – as preached, and as witnessed by Thurman's grandmother – had little to do with such affairs of this world as health, poverty, justice, human dignity. Rather, this Jesus, as preached, moved very swiftly from being a helpless little baby to being a helpless saviour crucified because of people's sins.

> The Jesus who said ' Blessed are the poor',
> the Jesus who came to liberate people from the strictures of a dominant minority power elite
> the Jesus who saw more faith in a non-Jew from the Mediterranean region than he saw in his own race
> the Jesus who was helped to carry his cross by a black man
> – this Jesus never got a look in.

Instead there was the favouring of the helpless baby and the saviour who died because of sins. There was, in white preaching, a preponderance of Old Testament legalism and pseudo-Pauline censoriousness.

The implication in all this was that by dint of their colour, black people were sinful.

They were allegedly descended from Ham, the son of Noah, whom his father cursed and destined to be a slave to his brothers. If they confessed their sinfulness, and paid deference to their masters as to Christ, all would be well, not in this world but in the next.

This is a reduction of salvation. This is a diminished Jesus.

The eclipse of Christ as liberator

What was conveniently hidden from the victims of such demeaning theology (and might I suggest from many whites as well) was the truth that from the beginning of his ministry until his crucifixion, Jesus delighted in liberating people from misconceived notions about sin, and from being tied in knots by petty legislation which the powerful invented in order to control the powerless.

Cone and many Latin American theologians have seen the cross not simply as the symbol of God's forgiveness. Rather they recognise how in the cross Jesus enters into physical solidarity with oppressed people, sharing their pain and confronting their oppressors with such effectiveness that his detractors had to get rid of him. He goes to the cross rather than avoids it. He enters into solidarity with the persecuted, revealing how death can be both the consequence of and punishment for a life of transparent goodness; but he goes also knowing that goodness is stronger than evil, as his resurrection gloriously affirms.

Have we missed this leitmotif in Jesus – his association with the rejects of the earth?

Remember John the Baptist's disciples do a double take when it is pointed out to them that the Messiah is not doing a Bible study with the rabbis, but sitting in the company of prostitutes and other sinners. And worse, he is not preaching at them, he's enjoying a meal with them.

Have we missed that – as in the healing of the man born blind in John's Gospel – it is not those who are accused of sin whom Jesus excoriates. It is their accusers. Thus he confronts Pharisees, the sin-sniffers par excellence, who believe that every deviation from the norm in terms of behaviour or health is caused by sin. To them he says:

'Because you say 'We see'
your sin *remains' (John 9:41)*

It was because Christ chose to self-identify with the wretched of the earth that he was crucified, because he claimed that those who were labelled sinners were less guilty than the ones who persecuted them. God, in raising him up, shows that salvation is not just from sin but from injustice. In the cross these two perspectives should not be separated. Thus those who believe themselves to be saved should be co-partners with Christ in his great work of liberation.

Perhaps I have too long focused on what has happened and been written in the USA. If so, it is probably because there is easier access to black theology there than in Britain. It is certainly not because this country is devoid of racism, not when there is a gross disproportion in the number of blacks over against whites who are stopped by the police in our streets, and not when there is a gross disproportion in the percentages of white and black people incarcerated in our prisons.

Our country and its administrators are not devoid of racism when citizens of the former colony called the USA can easily visit Britain, but if you come from a Commonwealth country like Kenya, you have to pay hundreds of pounds for an interview in Nairobi to attest your worthiness. Then, if you are deemed suitable, your application has to be formalised and your visa issued in South Africa which, as with friends of mine, means that you might get your travel documents a few days after your plane has left.

We are a nation whose long history of colonialism and political interference in every continent should encourage a certain humility, not to say hospitality, towards those whose nations we once controlled.

Think of the current major troubled regions of the world – Northern Nigeria, Uganda, Zimbabwe, Afghanistan, Iraq, Iran,

Syrian, Libya, Palestine, Yemen.

What do they have in common? They were either colonised by Britain or have known British interference in their political life.

Our country and its government are not devoid of racism ... not when legislation enacted by a previous Home Secretary adversely affected over 5,000 people whom Britain invited to leave the West Indies in the '50s and '60s to take up employment here. The legislation (since repealed) destined them, if they had not secured a UK passport, to be returned to their country of origin despite having lived, worked and paid taxes in Britain for decades.

Is there a dormant racist gene within those of us who are born white?

The Cambridge academic Priyamvada Gopal would say so, having been repeatedly the victim of racial profiling by suspicious porters in that revered establishment's colleges. She works in a university which asserts its openness to people of colour by boasting that it admitted sixty – *sixty* – black UK students in 2017. At that very time the student population numbered 21,656.

We cannot follow Jesus if all we do is celebrate his birth as a helpless baby and his death as a helpless saviour on the cross whose primary concern is in delivering the socially compliant from their sins. You cannot be a disciple of such a skinny saviour whose celebrated characteristics are that he was 'gentle, meek and mild' – a trinity of adjectives gloriously absent from the Gospels. This is a diminished Jesus.

To be a disciple is – among other things – to join with Jesus in his incarnate ministry of solidarity with and liberation of those unjustly oppressed. And perhaps in the present fraught climate where populist politicians like Trump and Johnson enjoy playing to the xenophobic gallery, we have to be more proactive as regards hospitality, inclusion and racial justice.

If people want to ask why I, a white man, am speaking out on this, it's because I have known the effect of similar prejudices.

Coming from a predominantly Protestant nation, in which Catholics were a demeaned community, I realised that it took Presbyterians four hundred years to repent of our prejudice, epitomised in a line in the Westminster Confession of Faith (which ministers have to subscribe to), which calls the Pope the 'anti-Christ'. Note also that in the predominantly Protestant province of Northern Ireland, it was not until the 1960s that the franchise in local elections was extended to Catholics.

I still have deep regret for ways in which my culture acquiesced to this discrimination.

Black people deserve evidence from their white counterparts that they repent of the ways in which the 'whitening' of Jesus was a deviant cultural appropriation which limited the inclusivity of the Gospel and demeaned non-Caucasian people, who were made equally in the image of God. It is when we open ourselves to perspectives on faith which come from previously subjugated people that we embrace and are embraced by a larger Christ.

God and women

But a bigger proportion of humanity – indeed over 50% of it – is similarly deserving of liberation from myths woven through the ages regarding God's preference for males.

Genesis – in God's image

Why has it taken me so long to come to terms with the fact that right at the beginning of the Bible, in Genesis chapter 1, it states:

> *God created human beings in his own image;*
> *in the image of God he created them;*
> *male and female he created them.*
> (Genesis 1:27)

Simple logic, which defies many of us, suggests that if both men and women are made in God's image, then it might take men and women working in concert to understand the mind and purposes of God. Instead we are inheritors of a traditional perspective which sees the male person as the noblest work of God, and the female person as a necessary but fallible appendage.

It has everything to do with the presumption that Eve led Adam into sin by offering him whatever fruit – apple or apricot – was hanging from the tree of the knowledge of good and evil – a perspective which Paul, but not Jesus, endorses. But there are perhaps three things overlooked by those who are forever keen to suggest that woman is God's afterthought and man's ruin.

The first is that it is only to Adam that the command not to eat the fruit is made. Eve is not present when the prohibition is made.

Secondly, she does not seduce Adam into eating it. She gives him some; she doesn't force it down his throat like a mother spooning cod liver oil into her resistant offspring.

Thirdly, when God asks Adam if he ate the forbidden fruit, he doesn't say yes or no. He says, 'It was my wife wot gave me it.'

Iranian Muslims

I could give any number of other examples where women have offered insights into the scriptures which men could never have fashioned. This extends to women who are not Christian.

One of my friends, a Canadian academic, was part of an exchange between a Christian college in Winnipeg and an Islamic seminary in Iran. When she taught in Iran, she introduced the students, both male and female, to some stories of Jesus familiar to Christians. One of them was the account of Jesus engaging with a Samaritan woman at a well. (*John 4*) As she read the narrative she noticed that the female Islamic students kept giggling. Being Middle-Eastern women, they could relate to the text in a way no

Western man could. They could recognise the mating presumptions within it, the ambiguity of the dialogue between Jesus and the woman. They saw it as a story in which the woman was not a shrinking violet but a girl with her eye on the main chance.

Eyes opened through re-reading the Bible

Realisations like this encouraged me to re-read the Bible in an unusual way. From Advent 2015 until Advent 2016, I gradually skim-read through the whole Bible from Genesis to Revelation, reading slowly only those chapters in which women were mentioned.

And I took note of their names.

At the end of the year, I was amazed at what I had found, but also annoyed with myself that I had hitherto been dismissive of a vast array of female heroes of the faith, women whom God had called, commissioned, inspired and encouraged to break the presumption of subservience which was dominant in their culture ...

Women such as
Dinah,
Jochebed,
Mahlah, Noah, Hoglah, Milcah and Tirzah,
Achsah
Merab
Abigail
Rizpah
Huldah

... what all of these have in common is that they are the victims of male discrimination and cruelty, but they did not stay silent.

I mention the quintet Mahlah, Noah, Hoglah, Milcah and Tirzah. These are otherwise known as the daughters of a man called Zelophehad. They make two appearances in the Hebrew Scriptures, both times in the book of Numbers, which is not everyone's idea of bedtime reading. (*Numbers 27:1-11 & 36:1-12*)

They are girls who are left in an awkward dilemma when their father dies. The law states that if a man died and he had no sons, his property and wealth should go to his brothers. The five girls think this is unfair so they go to complain to Moses. They say that they did not ask to be girls, nor did their father ask for daughters. Had they been boys, they would have been his heirs, but being girls with no brothers, they will now be dependent on and controlled by the inheritors of their father's property, namely their uncles.

Moses has no immediate answer for these harpies, so he decides to take it to the Lord in prayer. And God says, 'Change the law, and give the girls their father's inheritance.'

This is three thousand years before the law of primogeniture was changed in Britain so that royal succession no longer goes to the first male child of the monarch but to the first child, irrespective of gender.

The discrimination against women and in favour of men percolates through Old Testament Law, such that it states that if a girl should be raped in a city and no one hears her cries for help, it will be presumed that she consented to the invasion of her body. (*Deuteronomy 22:23-24*)

When Jesus appears on the stage of history, he comes to 'fulfil what was spoken of him in the law and prophets and psalms'. To fulfil does not mean to endorse but to express in its fullness. Thus we see in Jesus a bias to women which is not paralleled in men of his day. Let me take one or two facts from the Gospels to exemplify my claim that Jesus was atypical in the way he dealt with and represented women.

The atypicality of Jesus

1) Treatment of women

There are twenty-two women with whom Jesus has a direct association. Luke's Gospel uniquely mentions eighteen out of twenty-two and makes unique reference to ten out of twenty-two.

Woman caught in an act of adultery (John 9:1-11)

Take the woman caught in adultery – one of several women about whom there is a degree of sexual intrigue. This is not a woman whose sins Jesus forgives. Jesus actually forgives far fewer people in the Gospels than we imagine. There are just two – the call girl who washes his feet with her tears, and the paralysed man carried to Jesus by his friends.

In the Temple he encounters the woman who was allegedly caught in adultery. I say 'allegedly' because being a woman her testimony would be invalid. Jesus never asks about the details of the allegation. He never asks her if she has done what she is accused of. Rather he asks the men if they have never done anything amiss. They claim she is a sinner, so he asks them if they have never sinned, and suggests that whoever is an innocent should fulfil the law by initiating the woman's death by stoning. He does not specifically refer to sexual sin, but in the context of this encounter, that is a possible implication.

The men walk away, the eldest first. Then Jesus asks, 'Has no one condemned you?' She says no. And he replies, 'Neither do I condemn you.' Is that because he is neutral to adultery? No. So what explains his lack of condemnation?

Is it perhaps that knowing how biased the Jewish law was against women, Jesus realised that she may have been compromised by the very men who, though shaking their heads as they walk away, may have buttoned up their trousers not long before. It is interesting that when Jesus, in more theoretical terms, 'fulfils' the law, he specifically changes the understanding of the law against adultery. That law always worked in favour of men, who from Adam onwards would blame the woman for being a seductress.

'You have heard it said ...' says Jesus, ' "Do not commit adultery." But I say to you, "If a man *(not if a person or a woman)* looks at a woman with a lustful eye, he has already committed adultery with her in his heart." ' *(Matthew 5:27-28)*

In other words, Jesus is less keen on having the law describe a sin which has already been committed, than instilling an ethic of respect and self-control which prevents an adulterous act from happening in the first place. Here the onus is not on the woman, but on the man.

2) *Inclusiveness of language*

If we but look for it, we find an amazing inclusiveness of language used by Jesus which allows women to see that they, who are made equally in the image of God, are worthy to be represented in appropriate metaphors and similes.

Admittedly the following examples do not fit well in our more egalitarian society, but allow for first-century Israel being very different.

Jesus talks about how *new wine* doesn't fit in old wineskins (a male image) but also that a *new patch* doesn't work on old cloth (a female image). *(Mark 2:21-22)*

He talks about *corn being scattered* over land (a male image) and of *yeast being mixed* through dough (a female image). *(Luke 13:18-20)*

He says that the kingdom of *God is like a shepherd* who goes in search of a lost lamb, and when he finds it he celebrates with a feast. *(Luke 15:1-10)*

And he says in the next breath that the kingdom of *God is like a woman* who goes in search of a lost coin, and when she finds it she calls in her friends and they have a party.

Why is it that we can see God depicted as a shepherd but are reluctant to see God prefigured in the woman? Is it our upbringing? What we have heard? Or what we have read? Or is there a dormant sexist bias in the way we read scripture? If so, let's stop diminishing Jesus.

To represent him properly is a matter of justice to God and to each other.

[1] *The Cross and the Lynching Tree*, by James Cone (Orbis 2011)
[2] *Strange Fruit* by Abel Meeropol, recorded in 1939 by Billie Holiday
[3] *The Black Christ*, by Kelly Brown Douglas (Orbis 1994)

Hard listening

I could only have an hour with Salaam Hannah last week. He's a Christian clergyman from Syria whose church has been destroyed, and half the population of his town has moved elsewhere to escape the violence.

Only an hour, so I asked him the question I often ask of people coming from places affected by war: 'What do we in the West need to know about your nation?' And he made the same reply as I had heard in the past when I asked the selfsame question of Avner Gvoryahu from Israel and Shehade Shehade from Palestine and Anna Zaki from Egypt. He said, 'Things are much more complicated than you imagine.'

And then he went on, not so much to give his analysis of the tragedy of Syria as to comment on Western attitudes. And it was not easy to listen to.

He said that from his perspective the West seems to think that democracy is the answer, but democracy has to grow up from the ground, not be enforced from outside. He asked whether nations which were major arms producers should expect to be welcomed as peacemakers and honest brokers in countries where their weapons are being used to kill.

He suggested that, for the West, overseas engagement seemed so often to be based on economic expediency in favour of the benefactor, but seldom was cultural or ethical expediency part of the process. And he asked whether we ever thought of the consequences of our actions – as when you support the overthrow of a dictator, only to discover that he was sitting on a hornet's nest, and that deposing such a kingpin does not guarantee peace.

Salaam spoke with no rancour, but with sadness as he questioned some of the suppositions which many of us hold true.

Later, I remembered the moment in Jesus' ministry when *he*

met a Syrian, a woman who asked him if he would heal her daughter. He demurred and referred to her race as 'dogs'. She questioned his language and then something in their conversation – perhaps her plain speaking from a context he knew little about – changed him. He felt for her pain and rather than dismiss her, he agreed to help her.

Having met people from both sides involved in the troubles in Northern Ireland and apartheid in South Africa, I am convinced that it is only when we drop our unquestioned presumptions and feel for the pain of the one we despise or disagree with that we begin to move towards peace. It will not be fully secured by military hardware or economic master-plans but by the less exotic arts of listening, thinking outside the box and empathy, however hard it is to imagine doing this right now.

Thought for the Day
3 October 2014

Buried treasure

There's a phrase which has become commonplace at the conclusion of a debate or report on a significant disaster, whether that be a rail accident or a financial collapse. And this phrase has echoed continuously since the publication of the Chilcot Report. Its four words are:

'Lessons will be learned.'

I sometimes wonder why, given the number of times that statement has been repeated, we are not a more perfect people. Maybe it's because the phrase has an inherent weakness. It suggests that there is always a correct procedure which, if followed, will yield positive results; but if abandoned will lead to mistakes. That holds for some things but not for all.

Many children go to piano lessons. But even if they get their fingering right and can play scales perfectly, that doesn't lead either to guaranteed success on the concert platform or to the development of a love for music. Many people who in their younger life spent years trying to learn Beethoven's *Für Elise* will agree. You cannot acquire musicality simply by going to piano lessons

Some people have expressed disappointment that the Chilcot report does not carry many lessons regarding the future. Maybe that's because things like statesmanship, political integrity or appropriate military engagement cannot be acquired simply by following rules. Such things are the fruits of wisdom. And wisdom is not the product of a course of instruction leading to a doctorate in philosophy. It is the mature reflection on perception, intuition and experience. And it tends not to speak in platitudes but to encapsulate a profundity in words all can ponder.

Jesus, whose Hebrew tradition espoused wisdom as one of the most precious gifts of God, was one of its greatest and most succinct expositors. Two of his observations, which I slightly paraphrase, seem to me to be particularly pertinent as we consider the findings of the Chilcot Enquiry.

The first is this:

> When a malign presence vacates a place, it may come back, and finding it clean go and find seven others to make the place even worse than before. *(Luke 11:25-26 paraphrased)*

That bleak observation is as pertinent to regime change in a village hall as much as in a nation.

The second concerns any endeavour, political or personal, which has ramifications affecting others:

> No one builds a tower without first counting the cost. *(Luke14:28)*

Here, as elsewhere, Jesus does not make intellectual conjectures, but offers deep perceptions on lived life. This is wisdom – neither a critique nor a solution, but a gift which comes from both heaven and earth. It is called in scripture nothing less than 'the darling and delight of God', something to be sought as if it were buried treasure.

Thought for the Day
8 July 2016

The sin that dare not speak its name

This is an almost verbatim record of what I said in a seminar at Greenbelt Festival in 2010. I believe it is as relevant today as it was then. I've given a lot of talks there in large marquees where there is always a buzz of conversation as the audience waits for the speaker. On that occasion, there was a pall of solemn silence as people gathered. Even before I spoke, people were weeping, and this continued throughout the fifty minutes for which I spoke. It felt like offering a tribute at the funeral of people who had been killed in a tragedy. I have never had a more difficult public engagement before or since.

Introduction

There are three things I want to say before I get into the substance of this seminar.

1) The first is that I have never spoken on the issue of child abuse before. And I regard it as certainly one of the most difficult – but also one of the most important – issues I have ever addressed.

   I do not speak out of the experience of ever having been in a situation of abuse either as a victim or perpetrator. But I have had many conversations with victims. And more recently I have had contact with people who are actual or potential offenders.

2) I anticipate that whatever I say here will be misunderstood by some people. I anticipate that some will presume that I am trying to make excuses for sex offenders. This is certainly not my intention. But I am aware that where people have had personal experience of abuse, or have known the horror others have suffered, then it is well nigh impossible to feel

anything other than revulsion when the issue of child sex abuse is raised.

3) Thirdly, I will not be taking questions at the end of this seminar. And this for one very simple reason. It has taken me weeks to prepare to speak on this issue in such a public forum. And I fear that the emotions stirred by this might lead people to make instant responses which could compromise either themselves or others.

Thought for the Day, 22 March 2010

Here is my starting point.

Occasionally I am asked to present *Thought for the Day* on Radio 4. The expectation is that presenters will take a current issue in the news and reflect on it from their professed religious perspective.

In the middle of March this year one of the current issues was a letter from the Pope to the Irish Roman Catholic Church. It came in the wake of a damning report by the Irish Government which indicted the church for failing to deal properly with both victims and perpetrators of sexual abuse. It happened that a week or so earlier I had been in Ireland where I met a priest who years previously had been a whistle-blower. He was aware that a senior colleague was abusing children. He reported this to his bishop, only to be told that he should say no more about it, and to that end he, the complainant, was moved to a different parish.

So I decided to deal with this issue and presented this script which I will read in full:

Just a glance at the Pope's pastoral letter to the church in Ireland is enough to confirm that it is lengthy, inclusive and detailed ... an exceptional document as several commentators have indicated. I think that if I were a priest in that church I'd go down on my knees before my congregation and ask for forgiveness ... and that not out of personal guilt. When an institution through its silence seems to condone child abuse, then all in leadership – including the innocent – realise that they share responsibility. Given the control which the Church in Ireland has long held over education, the degree of potential contact between aberrant priests and innocent children has been considerable. *However, it would be wrong to think that child abuse is a phenomenon specific to religious establishments.*

Years after I had left employment in child care for a London borough, I returned to my previous workplace and enquired after former colleagues who had worked in other children's homes. I was astounded to discover that some of them, who had seemed the most decent of men, were serving time for abusing those in their care.

If child abuse is a phenomenon which won't go away, then it is right that those in close contact with children should be screened. But screening doesn't eradicate desire ... and it's the desire or temptation to abuse children which needs more attention. We have signs in public places telling people what to do if they suspect they have a propensity towards alcoholism. But what do you do if you suspect you are a paedophile?

At university in the '70s, I was elected president of the Students' Representative Council at a time when my university had no counselling service. One day a 20-year-old student came into my office and asked if he could speak to me. He first told me that he felt called by God to the priesthood. And then he said that he wanted to admit to a sexual attraction to children.

'Why are you telling me this?' I asked. 'Because,' he said, 'I can't keep this secret any longer. It's too dangerous. I need to tell somebody. And I need to promise somebody that I will never, ever harm children.'

What would you have done? I never knew his name. Had he said he was a sex offender, my response would have been clear and *straightforward. But this was different. He had somehow found the courage to admit to a potential he swore he would never pursue.*

Punishment after the event is not enough. Children will have been hurt. Yet we can't castrate or criminalise people who admit that there is within themselves a tendency they never wanted to be born with. Is it possible to affirm the potential for good that is in them, while holding them accountable for ensuring that they are the only ones who will ever deal with their inner demons?

Reactions

Sometimes people write in response to *Thought for the Day* presenters … not always politely. So I had one letter from an ardent Protestant who felt that I had not been bold enough in putting in the boot as regards the Catholic Church.

Another response came from a woman who accused me of being a rapist. By the nature of her very incoherent letter, I concluded that she had a serious history of abuse which had left her severely psychologically scarred.

There were also three letters, much more subdued in tone, which came from men, two of whom wrote with great appreciation that the issue had been aired. Both had similar stories. When they were in their early twenties, they had recognised that they had a dangerous sexual attraction to young children. They realised the criminality involved should they pursue their desires, and they knew intrinsically that this kind of activity was morally wrong in any circumstances.

Both sought help and both found help. And both went on to get married, have a family and never engaged in any sexual way with children. One – a man now in his seventies – said that the awareness of his desire never went away, though its intensity diminished with time. Both were examples of men who acted on their self-awareness and thereby prevented untold suffering to children and to themselves.

But there was another letter from a man who is, I subsequently discovered, now in his mid-thirties. He wrote from the prison in which he is serving a ten-year sentence for child abuse. His letter was in some ways the most moving, because he did not for a moment want sympathy or to try to rationalise his behaviour or say that he had been wrongly convicted.

He said very clearly that his sentence was just and justifiable because what he had done to a child was despicable. Then he commented that when in his late teens he realised that he was sexually attracted to young children, he tried to seek help. But he was never given any.

I'll say that again: *When in his late teens he realised that he was sexually attracted to young children, he tried to seek help. But he was never given any.*

Asking the professionals

Gradually I have understood why. Prior to my broadcast and after it, I spoke to a range of professional people to whom I asked the question: What would you do if someone approached you and said, 'I want to talk to you because I know that I am sexually attracted to children.' This, as I mentioned in *Thought for the Day*, had once happened to me when I was president of the Students' Representative Council at Glasgow University.

I asked a psychotherapist who said, 'I don't know what I would do. It has never happened. I only see such people after they have offended.'

I spoke to a doctor who gave a similar response.

I spoke to a social worker and a school headmistress, both of whom said, 'I would report him.' When I asked, 'To whom?' they said, 'The police.' When I said, 'But what if he had never done anything?' they were both stumped. They automatically assumed that admitting to the desire was proof of past guilt.

I then spoke to an academic, a very fond and trusted friend of mine with whom I used to work closely, a woman who had done extensive research on abused women.

After I asked the question, there were about two minutes of silence. And I realised what was happening ... as had been the case with some of the other people I had spoken with and have spoken to since. The horror which the phenomenon evokes – especially if you have been abused – is so intense that it is impossible to think with a calm mind about someone who has that malign potential ... even if he or she has never exploited it.

And we have a right to be horrified ... Because the statistics are horrifying

Horrifying statistics

It is now commonly reckoned that between 20 and 40% of children experience some form of sexual violence before the age of 18. More specifically, between 10 and 20% of boys will have been the victims of sexual abuse or sexual menace before the age of 18. With girls it is more horrific. Between a third and a half of girls will have experienced actual or intended sexual abuse before the age of 18.

Between 80% and 95% of abuse is initiated by men. Over 75% of abusive acts will be perpetrated by relatives or authority figures – such as teachers, clergymen – in whom the victim has a measure of trust.

And it is reckoned that the conviction rate for child abuse is only 1%.

Prevention of offending?

But what, for me at least, is equally horrifying is that virtually no one speaks of measures to prevent the potential abuser from offending. All the eggs go into the basket of child protection and the severe punishment of offenders.

Men can read in gents' toilets of how, if they have xyz symptoms, they might have gonorrhoea, diabetes or alcoholism, for which reason they should phone this or that helpline.

Most people now know that if they should feel suicidal, they need only dial the Samaritans and thus will be able to speak in complete confidence to someone who may be able to prevent them from self-harming.

But what if you think you might abuse a child? Where is the helpline to prevent such an eventuality? Instead, the demonisation of abusers is so ferocious that people who realise they have a propensity to offend are scared out of their wits to seek help. They fear disclosure, but by keeping secret their desire, they become ever more dangerous, because the desire can intensify rather than abate.

Now if someone should be asking, 'But what has this to do with faith or the church?', I have to say it has everything to do with faith and the church. This is not simply because in recent years we have seen admissions of guilt and negligence on the part of

- The Roman Catholic Church in the USA and Ireland
- The Anglican, Mennonite and United Churches in Canada
- Several denominations in Australia
- and the Anglican and Roman Catholic Churches in the United Kingdom.

Religion, even born-again religion, is no inoculation against this malign potential, and indeed because the churches have been gloriously silent for centuries on the issue, potential offenders have found the church something of a safe place in which to indulge themselves.

Over twenty years ago, when the Orkney Child Abuse investigations brought the issue to national prominence, I was asked by a minister if I would lead an evening service in which I might explore this burning topic of the day. I decided to do this and to focus the attention of the congregation through scripture and prayer on the problem of child abuse.

During the service, three women walked out. Two weeks later the minister phoned me to say that he had been in touch with each of them. Their reason for leaving was that each had been sexually abused by different men in the congregation who were in church that evening.

So let me do three things:

1) Offer some perspectives on the phenomenon

2) Ask why men especially engage in this

3) Ask how the Christian faith addresses or responds to it.

1) Perspectives on the abuse of children

Church as the main social work/educational agency

The reason why in Ireland, the USA and Canada the Church has so often been named in association with failing to address child abuse is partly historical. In these countries in the 19th and 20th centuries there was not even a nascent welfare state. The Church built and ran schools (almost 95% in Ireland), founded hospitals and universities, organised poor relief and ran orphanages. It did what in the UK is regarded as the government's job. So where the Church was the sole or main provider of childcare, if abuse took place it would be on church premises, as there were few other premises.

More particularly, with regard to the Roman Catholic Church it is only in retrospect that the dangers of the preferred pathway to the priesthood (junior seminary, senior seminary then ordination) have been realised.

In general this removal of children from a family unit at the age of puberty meant that these fledgling priests were never exposed to regular family life as were their secular peers. Nor, with few exceptions, was there much reflection in most seminaries about the implications of celibacy except that such a sacrifice of bodily passions was a means of honouring Christ.

Over twenty years ago, two American authors, Burkett and Bruni, published a book called *A Gospel of Shame* [1] which looked carefully at Catholic priests and paedophilia. They interviewed counsellors of paedophile priests and concluded that their actions did not result from the accessibility of young boys to them. The priests' sexual attraction to boys was present before ordination. It was their hope, I quote, 'that the mere act of ordination would trigger a mystical transformation that would lift their desires'.

But there's something more, for which I have to acknowledge my indebtedness to a very weighty tome called *The Puzzle* [2] by Louis A. Berman.

Berman produced an encyclopaedic study of homosexuality involving personal testimonies as well as published research. In his studies, he discovered that *The New Catholic Encyclopaedia* [3] of 1967 offered two suggestions as to why a homosexual man should consider the priesthood as a vocation. The first was that 'with the help of grace' the individual might find the power to overcome his tendencies through religious devotions. The second was that sheer devotion to the service of God and humanity might make no room for erring.

I am not for a moment saying that every homosexual priest is or ever was a paedophile. But if the issue of homosexuality has never been fully discussed with potential ordinands, then to spiritualise it as an aid to priestly service is dangerous.

A vocabulary of the body for children

Until relatively recently, children did not have a vocabulary which would enable them to speak easily about their body and specifically their genital regions. They were also taught to respect adults, particularly in church circles. One victim of whom I read was taught in Sunday School to honour her father and mother ... hours before her father routinely dishonoured her. With no vocabulary about her 'private parts' and with a reverence for her parents instilled in her, what could she do?

No mandatory awareness training in past years

In state establishments as much as in the Church there was, until comparatively recently, little said about 'boundaries' in looking after children. Childcare was a job for which there was little by way of vocational training ... until around thirty years ago.

I know this because in the 1970s I worked for a London borough in a hostel for boys aged between 14 and 18. They were in care, some because they were orphaned and too old for children's homes, some because they were the offspring of Windrush generation parents who could not deal with their urbanised progeny, some because of court orders.

I remember one morning being on duty with another member of staff. We had to waken the boys, and get them out of bed and down to breakfast by 8 o'clock. It was never the most pleasant of tasks. I had done the initial round of opening doors and wakening the boys, and then went on a second round to ensure they were up.

I went into a room where the sole occupant was a 15-year-old boy whom we'll call Robin. He was standing in front of a mirror admiring his large erect penis. He said, 'What would you do with this, Mr Bell?' I said, 'If I were you I'd put it in my pocket and come down and have your breakfast.'

Had I been a potential abuser, nothing in my engagement for that job would have signalled a red light. One of my brothers also worked for three years in the same London borough in a home for younger children. I asked him whether anyone had ever spoken to raise issues of sexual abuse or boundaries of behaviour with children. Nothing had been mentioned.

This is not to make excuses ... but to give a historical context.

2) Why do men (particularly) engage in child abuse?

I dearly wish someone could give definitive information regarding this. I have read several books, but all deal with men after the event. No one seems to be dealing with the rogue element within certain men. From what I can glean, there are multiple factors.

If you ask, 'Are people born this way?', at the moment I would say no. Or if they are, it is a very small percentage. Perhaps if it were a genetic disorder, more attention would be paid to those so affected. But so far no rogue gene in the DNA has been discovered.

Here are other considerations:

Abusers who were abused

Many people – at their most generous – might suggest that those who abuse have themselves been abused. They reckon that they are tainted and in an attempt to free themselves they pass it on ... as in a game of tig. Or it might be that, having been damaged by abuse, they try to deal with that damage by inflicting a similar wound on someone else. Taking revenge on an innocent victim.

Certainly I remember years ago being asked if I would spend

time with a young man in his mid-twenties who was severely psychologically damaged. It transpired that in the '60s he had lived in a house about 200 yards from where I then stayed in Glasgow. For four years, between the ages of 9 and 13, he had been systematically abused by his father, uncle and aunt while films were made. They were junkies and this is how they got money for drugs.

When I met him he had come back up from London to which he had run away years previously. He had met up with a girl, and they had a daughter. When he was 25 and the daughter was 8, the young man – call him Gordon – felt an impulse to sexually abuse her. Fortunately he was already under psychiatric care. So he mentioned this to his psychiatrist and he was able to take action to avoid any offence.

But not all victims become paedophiles. And not all paedophiles are previous victims. A social worker specialising in abused children told me recently that 95% of people who are abused do not go on to abuse others.

Last year a First Nations leader in Canada conjectured that because of the high rates of historical abuse, particularly in educational establishments, the knock-on effect was so considerable that if people were to be prosecuted for child abuse, some villages would see most of their populations imprisoned.

Most of us grow up with a gradual dawning of genital and sexual awareness which will mature through adolescence and into our teens. But if we have had invasive sexual experiences before, say, the age of 11, our sense of what is appropriate will be totally askew, and that lack of sensitisation may be a contributory factor in child abuse.

Other demeaning childhood experiences

I spoke earlier this year to a 37-year-old man in the USA who is attracted to boys. Whether or not he has abused any he would not say. But he did admit to an attraction. I asked him whether he was aware that to indulge himself would be both a moral and criminal act, and he admitted he was aware of that.

Then I asked what he believed was the root of his fascination with adolescents. He began to talk about his childhood. He had never been abused, but he had been bullied by people his own age when he was going through puberty. He had been very unhappy and ever since had been distrustful of people of his own age.

He felt that he could connect more easily with adolescents and they with him. It was as if he was trying to re-live years of his life which had been clouded with hurt and anxiety. This was a constant rather than an occasional passion, to explore with adolescents what had been forbidden him when he was their age.

Alastair's testimony

But let me read from the letter I received last week from the man in prison whom I mentioned earlier who is serving a ten-year sentence. We'll call him Alastair. I wrote asking if he could help me by answering some questions and promised that while I would never disclose his identity, I might quote from any reply he might send.

He wrote a long, and at times painfully moving, letter. From this I quote:

> *In response to your question about my attraction to children, let me give you some background.*
>
> *From a very early age I experienced strong sexual feelings towards other children, mostly boys. These (feelings) manifested themselves in behaviour from touching to more serious sexual acts; all this was between the ages of 4 and 12.*
>
> *When in secondary school, the dynamics of my relationships changed – perhaps a fear of being found out and being branded as gay, or of being reported to my parents – and so the activity*

ceased. This was how things were until my early twenties. I did not have a relationship with girls at school. I knew I was gay, but coming out was not an option. The school environment made me feel like a second-class person. I managed reasonably well in academic terms, yet I failed to mature as regards emotions, relationships and boundaries. As my teenage years went by, I think I used recollections from my childhood as my sexual reference point.

This is a rather long way round to say that there was no specific incident or point in time, but rather a failure to mature beyond the behaviour of my early years.

However, there was a trigger in the mid-90s when thoughts were pushed into my mind via access to the internet. Although I did not seek out inappropriate images, it was not long before I found numerous places in which to find such pictures. Looking back now I think that I often saw myself as the child in the image. I find this a frightening revelation. Maybe that is why I found myself seeking older men for anonymous sex, sometimes quite violent, sometimes for money.

James Newton Poling, an American pastoral theologian who has written on this issue,[4] recognises from his work with offenders certain common traits … though it seems to me that these may be the results of abuse rather than pre-existent conditions. They are:

– A sexualisation of dependency … a need to be needed which leads to inappropriate intimate behaviour.

– Destructive aggression … a need to get frustration out of the system, and doing that by picking on a weaker being.

– A narcissistic disorder … believing that he or she is so perfect and important that every desire, base or otherwise, should be fulfilled.

– An inability to respect limits ... which might be the result of being spoiled as a child by a parent or parents who were afraid to say no.

Androcentric structures

But along with this there is undoubtedly something about men, who constitute the vast majority of actual and potential offenders. Poling and other people recognise that there are too many androcentric (male-centred) structures which are presumptive of men being in power – the worlds of finance, business, industry, politics as well as the church witness to this.

Remember how in a recent government trade mission to India, of the sixty glitterati rooting for the UK, only four were women.

The sexist presumption in popular advertisements that women are weaker, and the recurrent images in pornography suggesting that women have to be mastered, nourish the assumption that men have constantly to exercise powerful responsibility.

Men have to prove they are in control. A frustrated man, or a man who cannot speak of his distressed emotional state, or a man who is sexually frustrated, is less likely than a woman to deal with his dilemma by sharing it with a friend. Instead he may internalise it until the suppressed anger or frustration cries out for expiation and the victim becomes someone obviously weaker ... a woman or a child.

Jewish-Christian incentives

For far too long the Jewish-Christian tradition has played along with this. Male headship of the family, let alone the church, has been conducive to it. And there are stories within the scriptures which – to a fevered mind – might be seen to give encouragement to a potential abuser.

One is the story of Abraham who loves both Ishmael and Isaac, yet is prepared to see the one starve and to sacrifice the other. *(Genesis 1:1-21)* Another is that of Lot who is prepared to send his daughters into the streets to satisfy the lusts of a crowd of men who want to have sex with the angels he has as house guests. *(Genesis 19:1-11)* Yet another is the story of Jephthah who, as the result of a casual oath to God, sacrifices his daughter who has barely reached adolescence. *(Judges 11:30-40)*

And there is that theory of the atonement which sees God as an angry father who is perturbed by the iniquity of his sinful children, a father whose anger will only be appeased if his son who is unblemished and sinless should die in the place of the guilty. And thereby atone for their sins.

If these things seem far-fetched, speak to a 'Christian' child abuser about his theology.

3) So how should we respond to this phenomenon?

How do we deal with this rogue desire in a proportion of all people, believers and non-believers alike, to sexually engage with young people. Let me make one or two suggestions. I offer these *not* as solutions or fully thought-out responses. They are themes offered for development and variation.

Stop the sexualisation of childhood

Three months ago I found myself curiously affected by two posters in the underground station near where I live in Glasgow. There were two almost androgynous figures – though on closer inspection, one was clearly male and the other female. They were modelling stylish clothes.

It must have been the third time I passed the poster that I realised that the clothes being modelled were typical of what seventeen- or eighteen-year-olds might wear. But actually the models could have been no more than seven or eight years of age.

What I noticed was not atypical of a move within advertising to seduce parents into purchasing clothes for children which will make them look more grown up. And if they are made to look more grown up, then they may be encouraged to act more grown up, and the process of sexualisation, rather than be enabled by gradual dawning of hormonal change and emotional desire, is turbocharged.

I'm sure no mother or father would consciously wish to make their child an object of desire for an adult predator. But if we insist in dressing them beyond their years, we steal childhood from them. Indeed we may even be exploiting them.

More recently, I listened to women speaking about the list of items on the market which were sold as 'must-haves' for girls – lip gloss for 5-year-olds, bras for 8-year-olds who had no signs of breasts. They accorded with what Rachel Williams asked in a recent article in *The Guardian*: *Why is our society grooming three-and four-year-olds to aspire to be a footballer's wife?*

Encourage an honouring of the body

We have to develop within children's and youth work healthy ways of giving thanks to God for the body.

If – and only if – we believe that bodies are important, if we believe that the dawning of sexual and gender awareness is a good thing, if we believe that the body is the temple of the Holy Spirit, then we should not speak of such things as if they were reserved business.

I wish I had realised this when I was a youth worker. I wish I had thanked God with teenagers for their bodies, for the changes in them, for the passion in them. And asked God to enable a cherishing of the body, a sense of its uniqueness and its importance, and prayed that the body be kept from both illnesses and people who might cause harm.

To tell children that they should avoid strangers is insufficient. We should also be able to give them such a sense of pride in their body that they feel able to repudiate anyone who comes too close. In Indiana there is a paediatric unit in which staff whom the young patients name as being especially helpful are given a Red Shoe badge. This began some years ago when one of the professors was treating a child suffering from a very rare terminal illness. Indeed, she was a medical curio. The little girl loved red shoes and asked if she could wear her red shoes in bed. The professor gladly assented.

One day a number of trainee doctors led by another consultant gathered round her bed and proceeded to pull back the blankets and undress her. To this man the 8-year-old said, 'You can't do that without asking my permission.' So the eminent surgeon sent away his entourage, apologised to the little girl and asked her permission. Children should be enabled to say no.

Raise the profile of child abuse in public (religious) discourse

Because of the rate of incidence of child abuse, it is totally unhelpful if it remains an issue which churches only deal with when a pastor is prosecuted as a paedophile. It has to be a subject which is sensitively handled in preaching (though most of the texts that could be used to refer to it are not in the regular calendar of readings) and also in prayer.

We should be able from time to time to specifically ask God's help for those who are the victims of sexual abuse and for those who feel tempted to harm children. If we can be specific about children who face hunger or abduction in rogue states in the global South, we can be specific about children in our nation whose lifelong well-being might be compromised by abusive behaviour at home.

Provide safe havens

Finally, in places where there are brave and compassionate people, we need to think about having safe havens for those who have offended and for those who feel they have a potential to offend. The former already happens. In England, a number of Quaker families play host to men who have come out of prison, to try to affirm their humanity, hold them accountable for the conduct of their lives, and let them enjoy human company.

A year ago I met a quite amazing Methodist pastor from America whose name is Irene. She was visiting Scotland from Texas where she presently works.

Her church was confronted with the dilemma of having to decide what to do with a man in the congregation who had been caught in a police sting. They knew that he looked at child pornography and a policeman lured him into agreeing to meet with what he believed was a 13-year-old girl. He was taken to court and put on probation. But the court made it clear that he could only go back to his church, where there were children, if invited.

So the pastor held discussions with her church leaders, with parents and others, and at a church meeting which was full of passionate and compassionate observations, the congregation agreed to invite the man back. They asked him to sign a covenant regarding his behaviour and ensured that he would be befriended by people with whom he could develop relationships of trust and encouragement.

Some people, a very few, indicated that they would leave the church for personal reasons. But Irene was amazed by the number of parents with children and older people who saw this as a defining moment.

One of the by-products of their decision was the raising of consciousness about the issue. People who had long been silent admitted to being abused. This has resulted in the setting up of a group in the church, with a qualified counsellor, for the victims of child abuse.

Here is a church which is seeking to both rehabilitate the offender and care for the victim.

What a risk! But also what an example!

The *Thought for the Day* broadcast which elicited response from two men who knew themselves to be potential offenders allowed me to make contact with possible violaters who, thank God, have never compromised the trust or defiled the body of a child. I remember thinking that it would be great if they were able to speak out to show that prevention can work. Then I realised that that would be impossible ... for no one in their family or in their circle of friends knows the private temptation they have had to deal with. They cannot go public. Nor can Alastair who is in prison partly because when he sought help there was no one to respond.

It is for them that I have spoken.

Afterword

It is over ten years since I delivered this talk. In the interim there have been few indications that prevention is being taken seriously. But I did find some hope in an organisation which, in Scotland, is called Stop It Now. Its staff includes former members of the police force and trained psychologists. When I visited their premises, they indicated that one of the triggers for some people is the ease with which child pornography can be sourced. I met two men, one of whom had been convicted and one who was facing con-viction, who had become addicted to child pornography. One said it was like a vortex which both held you in its grasp and created a desire for more and more horrendous images. Both also said that they were glad they had been caught, for they did not know how they could have freed themselves.

On occasions when I have tried to raise the issue of child sex abuse in religious circles, I have not found much encouragement. People in official positions often blanch at the prospect, but – as I discovered in a Liverpool parish – people on the ground are less likely to shy away from it.

Indeed, as I write, BBC television is presenting a series of three programmes, entitled *Football's Guilty Secret*, which involves the testimonies of several of the hundreds of former amateur and professional players who, in their adolescent and early teenage years, were compromised, abused and raped by coaches, all of whom seem to have been married.

I close with a text written for a church in a deprived area of Sydney, Australia. Aware of the high incidence of child abuse in the surrounding area, they held a service to enable those who had been victimised, and those who care for the victims, to lay out before God and each other the pain of it all, and pray not for peace but for justice.

We Sing for Those Whose Song is Silent

1. We sing for those whose song is silent,
   whose hidden hurt no tune could bear –
   children whose innocence of loving
   has long since gone beyond repair.
   God, who conceived and gave us birth,
   listen for those who've lost their worth.

2. We sing for those whose lives were mangled
   when friendship turned to vile abuse,
   as those they trusted traded kindness
   for cruelty beyond excuse.
   God in whose image all were made
   feel for the ones who've been betrayed.

3. We sing for those who bear within them
   scars in the body, mind and soul,
   fears from the past and, for tomorrow,
   yearnings that they might yet be whole.
   God who in Christ was touched by pain,
   make your hurt children whole again.

4. We pray for those who know temptation
   worse than our earnest words can tell,
   who covet power, who lie in waiting
   with evil lusts designed in hell.
   Jesus through whom the world is saved
   conquer the sin, heal the depraved.

5. We sing that through believing people
   lives may be hallowed and made good,
   and ask that God in every victim
   shall see faith, hope and love renewed.
   This is our prayer, this is our song
   to God, to whom we all belong.[5]

[1] *A Gospel of Shame: Children, Sexual Abuse and the Catholic Church* by Frank Bruni & Elinor Burkitt. Perennial 2002
[2] *The Puzzle: Exploring the Evolutionary Puzzle of Male Homosexuality* by Louis Arthur Berman. Godot 2003
[3] *The New Catholic Encyclopaedia*. McGraw-Hill 1967
[4] *The Abuse of Power* by James Newton Poling. Abingdon Press 1991
[5] *We Sing for Those Whose Song is Silent* by John L. Bell, copyright WGRG. The Iona Community 2014

Another substantial book which deals with the issue of paedophilia is *Erotic Innocence* by James R. Kincaid. Duke University Press 1998

Poetry in slow time

Having travelled from the south to the north on New Year's Day, when I got home I relaxed in a comfortable chair with a cup of tea and turned on the radio. I recognised the voice first: it was that of Jeremy Irons. But I did not recognise the TS Eliot poems he was reading. Texts such as *Animula* and *The Cultivation of Christmas Trees* were not ones with which I was familiar. But as I listened I realised that I rarely heard the whole poem. Rather one word or phrase like 'the drug of dreams' would draw me into thoughts or memories, into an inner world which I had not visited for some time.

I enjoyed hearing the more familiar *Journey of the Magi*, a poem about the Wise Men coming to see the infant Jesus. But afterwards I spent a long time thinking about how, for these men, this birth which they came to celebrate was, as Eliot suggested, like a death – a death of old systems, old beliefs, old understandings of what God and the world were about.

Poetry does that. It slows us down. It makes us think. We can't race through it. I can happily spend an hour or two reading a novel, turning page after page, trying to get to the end of a long chapter before I lay the book down. But I would never read fifty pages of poetry in one go. Poetry demands a different kind of attention. It only delivers of itself the more we let the words seep into us.

This realisation has changed the way I read the poems in the Bible called the Psalms.

Rather than treat them as historical narratives, I read them slowly, feeling for what connections there may be between the writer's experience and my own and toying playfully with the natural as well as the mental images. One day I got a surprise when I was reading the best known psalm in the world, Psalm 23, which I remember my grandmother singing to me when I was only two years old.

It begins 'The Lord is my shepherd' – a very pastoral image of God. But halfway through the image changes. 'You have spread a table for me.' It was only in pondering these words that I realised in this five-versed poem we have two images of God. At the time of writing and in many places even now, the shepherd and the table setter would be suggestive of predominantly male and female roles.

So this year, starting today when the demands of work and business become all-important again, I have decided in the face of breaking news and instant messaging to read poetry – both sacred and secular – slowly, as a reminder that truth is not the same as either factual information or emotional reaction … and that life was meant to be deep and not shallow.

Thought for the Day
3 January 2017

Historic Schottische

One wintry night in 1972, I was sitting on the top deck of a number 38 London bus heading towards Balls Pond Road. A fellow countryman, clearly the worse for wear, stood up at the front and began to assail the passengers with a litany of questions to which he also gave the answers:

Who was it who gave you yer steam engine? A Scotsman!
Who was it who gave you yer telephone?   A Scotsman!
Who was it who gave you yer television?   A Scotsman!
Who was it who gave you yer penicillin?   A Scotsman!

And then, as he was catching his breath, a voice from behind called out, 'And who was it who gave you your whisky?'... to which everyone on the upper deck chorused, 'A Scotsman!'

This is St Andrew's Day, Scotland's patronal festival when, pray God, few of us will visit that kind of interrogation on others. Far from educating Londoners, the man on the bus was displaying both ignorance and prejudice, maybe because fifty years ago, as a nation, we had low self-esteem. We actually didn't know much about ourselves.

Despite studying history at school, I was unaware that we became part of the United Kingdom largely because our attempt at colonising Panama bankrupted the nation and we had to be bailed out by England. Nor did I know that Scotland had freely participated in the slave trade. At one time we owned a third of the plantations in Jamaica. Nor was I made aware that in the 19th century lowland bailiffs were used by absentee landlords to evict Gaelic-speaking crofters from their ancestral lands and send them on ships across the Atlantic.

But I also didn't know that in the 13th century we had, in Duns Scotus, a theologian of the stature of Thomas Aquinas; in the 16th century we had, in Robert Carver, a composer as skilled and prolific as Palestrina; and in the 19th century we had a diaspora of entrepreneurs scattered across every continent. So, in the absence of a bigger picture, it was easier to develop a negative, partisan mentality which made us proud that we were not English, and we were not posh.

One of my favourite lines in the Gospel is where Jesus condenses his ethical teaching into a simple maxim: 'You shall know the truth, and the truth shall set you free.'

There is no aspect of life in which that truism fails to liberate – and most certainly when it comes to dealing with our prejudices, our ignorance and our fallible self-esteem.

Thought for the Day
30 November 2018

Celtic perspectives on death and dying

Twice in 2016 I was asked to speak at international gatherings in Scotland concerned with death and dying. I have no idea why. It is not because people in Scotland die with a greater frequency than people elsewhere. Here, we usually do it once.

While the first conference was mainly concerned with the care of the dying, the second had asked for some 'Celtic' perspectives on issues surrounding death. I had to do a little digging, as there was no authoritative source that came to mind. Too much that is said with regard to the Celtic tradition reflects a kind of saccharine spirituality which our progenitors would not recognise as an authentic expression of their faith.

The following are extracts from the lecture delivered to the Conference of the International Work Group on Death, Dying and Bereavement held at Dunblane on 8th November 2016.

A divided nation

Scotland is a small country. It has a population of 5.3 million people. In most places, if you drove fifty kilometres east or west, you would end up in the sea. It has four ancient and around twelve modern universities, but no great academic or ecclesiastical pedigree when it comes to discussion of death and dying, apart from notable work done by chaplains in some of our hospices.

More significantly for our purposes, there have been and still are two major divides in Scotland. These are not political. This is not the USA where every decision, whether at the level of national government or a local church, seems to be politicised. No, the divides are cultural.

The Highlands & Islands and the Lowlands.

The Highlands & Islands (to the north and west of the country) have always been more rural than the south, with few towns of more than 50,000 people. These lands were the site of forced expulsions in the 18th and 19th centuries when poor people were driven from their rented habitations by absentee landlords in order to make way for sheep or deer. Until the 19th century, in many parts of the Highlands & Islands the dominant language was Gaelic – a tongue which bears no resemblance to any other major language in Europe, but which is found in different variants among the rural populations of Scotland, Ireland, Wales and the very south-west of England.

Many of the Gaelic-speaking people in Scotland prior to the 20th century were illiterate – which is to say they could not read or write. But they were highly intelligent, very communitarian, and greatly creative, particularly in poetry and music. They were also the object of persecution when their music – particularly bag-pipe music – was forbidden by the British government and their native language was suppressed.

The Lowlands stretch south from the central belt between Glasgow and Edinburgh to the border with England. In this area traditionally most wealth resided, most universities were established, and the biggest cities and townships were located. Here, from the 18th century, most trade, industry and commerce have found their home, and here, since the Reformation, most people have been educated and literate in English, the predominant language.

Protestants and Catholics

Until 1540, Scotland was an exclusively Roman Catholic country. The mediaeval church was judged to be corrupt through wealth and privilege; it also had a dominant influence on the ruling monarchs.

Between 1540 and 1560, the Scottish Reformation took place. Unlike the Lutheran Reformation in Germany or the Anglican Reformation in England, the Scottish Reformation was intent not simply on reforming but also on replacing; it had as much an effect on the culture and politics of the nation as on its religious life.

The main leader of the Reformation, John Knox, a disciple of John Calvin, was an iconoclast. He ensured the destruction of corrupt government as well as the destruction of the aesthetic legacy of the past: no more bishops, no more Mass, no more fine music, no more paintings, statues or stained glass. And because the Queen (Mary) was a devout Roman Catholic, no more intervention from the monarch in the affairs of the nation.

And, to some extent, no more private spirituality. Instead, the close monitoring of personal faith and practice by a quasi-judicial body of men in every parish.

On the positive side, Knox was committed to universal education. Thus the building of schools as well as churches in every parish ensured that by the end of the 17th century, Scotland had a more literate population than England. It had four universities to England's two, despite England having ten times the number of inhabitants.

The Protestantisation of Scotland was affirmed by law in 1690 when the Presbyterian tradition became the 'established' church. At this time, therefore, in a nation of probably no more than one million people, we have two major divisions:

a) the cultural and linguistic division between the Lowlands and the Highlands & Islands

b) the religious division between the vast majority of the population who had become Protestant and a minority who especially in the Highlands & Islands held, albeit in secret, to Catholicism.

These divides remain to this day, though in different proportions. The north and especially the Northern Isles are not as impoverished as before, having flourished financially due to the exploitation of North Sea oil. And as regards religion, the re-establishment of the Roman Catholic hierarchy and the influx of immigrant populations from Ireland and the continent of Europe have helped to change the demographic of the Catholic Church so much that now it is reckoned that more people regularly attend Mass than attend worship in the Protestant churches.

Before I come to the word 'Celtic', I'd like to give just a snapshot of what happened in some places as regards death and dying before and after the Reformation.

Before

Prior to the Reformation, there were rituals which surrounded death. These included prayers said around the bed of the person who was dying, and anointing with oil, elsewhere referred to as final unction or the last rites.

After death people sat in the presence of the body, praying for the soul of the deceased. The body might be left at home for one or two or more nights – as long as it took to dig the grave and assemble mourners. On subsequent nights there might be wakes consisting in the telling of stories, the saying of prayers and the imbibing of alcohol.

While this happened in the home, in some small towns and villages three different bells were also rung – one to invite prayers for the dying, one to indicate the death and invite gratitude for the life, and one to encourage prayers for the mercy of God.

On the day of the funeral, the keening of women was a dominant feature. Keening was in some places an artform. It was a semi-musical improvisation in which the person's history might be rehearsed, their family might be named, the loss to the community spelt out and their journey to heaven commended. There might also be a requiem Mass, depending on the wealth of the family, and as the body was carried to the graveyard, a handbell would be rung to encourage people to join the family for the funeral and also to take turns at carrying the bier on which lay the deceased.

After

... and then the Reformation came and most of this changed. Here is a Church of Scotland decree of 1640:

> *When any person departs this life, let the body on the day of burial be decently taken from the house to the public graveyard, and there interred immediately without any ceremony.*[1]

There are no prayers for the deceased. There is no tolling bell. There will be no priest or minister at the grave, and certainly no women there.

There might be a service in the church before the burial, but no more. And in the Protestant Gaelic-speaking regions – as even today – the funeral oration might hardly refer to the person who has died. No tributes from friends or colleagues, but perhaps a solemn address from the minister to remind mourners of the fires of hell which await them unless they change their ways.

According to some scholars, right into the 19th century it was deemed reprehensible for a Protestant minister to bury the dead. There is a record from 1850 of how a minister in the south of Scotland was publicly chastised for holding a funeral service in the local graveyard. The suggestion made was that he was 'going post-haste to Rome'.[2]

A remnant or an echo of this was evident in the way I was trained in theological college.

I was told to pray for the person who was dying, but once he or she died I should have nothing more to do with the body but should then pray for the family. I was certainly not to pray for the repose of the soul of the deceased, nor even to touch the body, whether by way of farewell or to anoint it with oil or sprinkle it with water. That was what the Catholics did.

Perspectives from Celtic spirituality

The Celtic tradition

The Reformation left Scotland suspicious of how to deal with the dead and dying, and also how to deal with personal devotions. When the Bible was first published in English, there was an expectation that it would be read in people's homes, perhaps in the morning before work, perhaps at the end of the week. This was sometimes done more out of fear than out of joy. But little was said or taught about personal piety, personal prayer and what we might call spirituality.

Indeed, I never heard the word when I was at a Protestant seminary. I think we presumed that spirituality was something that Catholic priests, monks and nuns had. We, on the other hand, had sexuality ... and plenty of it. Thus, when I began working in 1978 and was encouraged to organise a conference on spirituality, the natural thing was to ask a Catholic priest to come and speak, which he – Fr Jock Dalrymple – did, to great effect.

Celtic ...

This word has an interesting history, because it does not belong to Scotland – or Ireland for that matter. The word Celtic comes from a Greek word *Keltoi* ... which was the name given to a tribe of people living in an area stretching from west-central France into Switzerland, south-western Germany and Austria, two thousand years before Christ. Most famously, Hallstatt in Austria has been the site of excavations which have uncovered remnants of a distinctive culture represented in their designs and artifacts, especially rings and ornaments.[3]

Historians now differ as regards the theories of how Keltoi ended up being a name associated with peoples as far apart as Galicia in north-western Spain and Galatia (to which St Paul wrote) in modern-day Turkey. Some espouse a theory of conquest and resettlement, others that their distinctive craftwork was gradually copied by the peoples among whom exiles from the Austrian region settled.

Five hundred years BC, some of these wandering people came over from north-eastern France to the south-west of England and particularly into Ireland where they intermarried with the local population and developed their craftwork.

Nine hundred years later, St Patrick came to Ireland and set up small monasteries and churches among these Celtic people. They had close associations politically with the western islands of Scotland and so, before long, these islands and some of the mainland nearby were referred to as Celtic.

Being remote from Rome and being primarily rural or island communities, the early faith collectives (hardly sufficiently organised to be called 'the Celtic Church') developed patterns of life and ministry which were at variance with mainstream Catholicism, including clerical marriage, a prominent role for women, and a date for Easter which was consonant with the Orthodox East rather than the Roman West.

There was also a higher degree of trust in and dependence on lay people. Priests could not be everywhere – they were itinerant, moving from settlement to settlement, where they encouraged the inhabitants to develop their own language of prayer, and even the taking on of some priestly duties.

Thus we discover that on the island of Barra there was an ancient tradition of what to do if a baby was born and there was no priest to baptise it. In such a case, neither the oldest inhabitant nor the community leader baptised the child, but the midwife, the one who had delivered the baby. She and her attending women celebrated the sacrament of baptism; it was an all-female ritual.

In illiterate populations – where no one could read or write Gaelic – wisdom, insight, song and spirituality were handed down from generation to generation and committed to memory in a way which is completely contrary to our present experience. We today are in danger of losing confidence in our ability to remember things, not because we suffer collectively from dementia, but because we rely on tablets and iPads, computers, memory sticks and satnavs to inform us of what we fear we might forget.

The ancient peoples and their descendants who were evangelised by the Celtic missions had very agile minds and, as with indigenous people all over the world, carried prayers, songs, gems of spiritual insight and nuggets of wisdom securely in their memories.

At the end of the 19th century, a scholar called Alexander Carmichael realised that because English was being imposed as the *lingua franca* on these Gaelic speakers, a lot of their inherited material, passed down through centuries, might be lost. So he set about systematically visiting villages and individual cottages, asking people what was precious for them which he could record for posterity. He filled five books with poems, prayers and wise sayings in Gaelic.

It happened also that in Ireland, at exactly the same time, a man called Wilfred Hyde began to do the same thing. And it is in the collected writings of these two that much of what nowadays is called Celtic Spirituality finds its origin.

That is not to deny the existence of earlier material from the saints and scholars. But their writing is found more prevalently in Ireland than Scotland, for the simple reason that the Scottish monastic settlements, such as Iona, were easy prey for Viking marauders. Iona Abbey was twice ransacked in the pre-Reformation period, but it was the Protestant reformers who destroyed the Benedictine abbey and church which had originally been erected around the first millennium.

It is only fragments of the writings of people like St Columba which have survived, and as regards the song or liturgy of the church, we know very little. The earliest pre-Reformation piece of liturgical music still extant is the Inchcolm Antiphoner of 1340.

So here I want to offer some of the perceptions which the ancient people held dear, such as may be gleaned primarily from what Alexander Carmichael recorded in the western Highlands & Islands.

Four perceptions

1) The Celts lived joyfully with mystery

There is no doubting the intelligence of the Celts. Their ability to think logically, to discuss intellectually, is clearly attested. But they did not believe that the life of the mind was all, that everything was reducible to inert data and logic. They believed – and had done since before Christianity came to Ireland – that the world was witness to and shot through with mystery.

Perhaps it is because people today spend so much time dealing with a barrage of facts, reading information posted on Facebook, looking for instant online answers for any question, solving every conundrum by reference to Wikipedia, that our openness to mystery has not only diminished but is satisfied by horror movies and science fiction.

Those who exist close to nature, who live by the seasons, who witness birth and death at first hand both in human and in animal life, those who watch the skies and observe beauty not as a plastic artifact but as a natural endowment within the created universe, have two reference points from which to ponder deep questions of life.

They have logic on one side and intuition on the other, reason on one side and experience on the other. Ditto for mental and spiritual intelligence.

This became abundantly manifest in a recent inquiry. It happened when a multinational mining conglomerate wanted to remove a mountain on the island of Harris and thereafter dig a super-quarry which would be one of the largest human-made holes in Europe. All of this was to be done in search of aggregate (stones) to enable road-building in continental Europe.

Among those who protested against this were two very different individuals. One was a Protestant professor of theology who had been born on the island of Lewis. His name was Donald MacLeod. The other was called Stone Eagle, the chief of the First Nations Mi'kmaq people in North America. Both spoke against the proposed super-quarry, not simply in economic or political terms, but in spiritual terms. Donald MacLeod expounded what I regard as a both original and succinct exposition of the relationship between Christian faith and ecology. Most memorably, he claimed that:

> 'Theologically, the primary function of the creation is to serve as a revelation of God. To spoil the creation is to disable it from performing this function.'[4]

The Celtic peoples lived and live with a sense of the numinous, the unseen mystery all around them. Life is not just logic. And for people of Christian faith, this extends to a belief in the presentness of heaven on earth, and of the people of heaven being constantly with us. The 'afterlife' for them is a continuation of the present life. It is our preference for sight over insight which prevents us which prevents us from seeing that we are part of eternity, not just time; and that we can invoke the solidarity of those in heaven to accompany us on earth.

Here are two night poems which affirm that neither sleep nor death is fearful because there are companions – Brigit, Mary, Jesus, angels – who are ever-present whether we are awake or sleeping or dying.

> *I lie down this night*
> *with Brigit of the mantles,*
> *with Mary of peace,*
> *with Jesus of the poor.*
>
> *I lie down this night*
> *with the nine angels,*
> *from the crown of my head*
> *to the soles of my feet.*[5]

The second poem – 'I lie down with God' – is one which I sometimes commend to people who have lost their life's partner, and who for the first time may be sleeping on their own.

> *I lie down with God*
> *and God lies down with me.*
> *I lie down with Christ*
> *and Christ lies down with me*
> *I lie down with the Spirit*
> *and the Spirit lies down with me.*
> *God and Christ and the Spirit – all three –*
> *with me.*[6]

The third poem, collected from a man who lived on the small island of Benbecula, enabled him every night to pray for his wife, his work, his safety and his death.

Bless to me the bed-companion of my love,
bless to me the handling of my hands.
Bless, O bless to me, the fencing of my defence,
and bless, O bless to me, the angeling of my rest. [7]

A contemporary expression of this openness to the mystery per-
petually around us is found in words of George MacLeod, the
founder of the present-day Iona Community to which I belong,
and who was largely responsible for the rebuilding of the monastic
buildings of Iona Abbey on the site where St Columba first established a monastery in 563.

In one of his prayers he writes:

In You all things consist and hang together:
the very atom is light energy
the grass is vibrant
the rocks pulsate.

All is in flux: turn but a stone and an angel moves. [8]

2) The solidarity of heaven and earth

Irrespective of what John Knox may have said and the fact that
the Presbyterian Church has always discouraged prayers for the
dead, the Celtic tradition claims most profoundly that death
should not lack its ceremonies.

In the ancient days, when a death was imminent, people would
recite the longest psalm in the Bible – Psalm 119, with 176 verses
– along with the Magnificat or Mary's song. Others, when the
Catholic Church had been re-established, would recite the Rosary
and the Our Father in the company of the one who was dying, for
good reason. If these words were known to the person when in
full health, then even in a pre-death subconscious state their reci-

tation might well provide comfort and remind them of the solidarity of friends who loved and revered these texts.

We do not know all that the seemingly unconscious mind is capable of realising. But we should not presume that an inert body presupposes an inert mind. One of my clerical colleagues recalls how he once visited a man in a coma on the same day every week. He would speak to him, tell him the news and always ended by reciting Psalm 23 and the Lord's Prayer. In time the man recovered consciousness and spoke of how when in the coma he had looked forward to his minister's visits and especially to hearing the two sacred texts said over him.

Today, people might go to a funeral or cremation service and afterwards never have a serious thought about the person who had died. But in the Columban tradition, there was an encouragement to name and remember and pray for the one who had gone. This, to some, might seem a waste of time, and to others a sign of love.

I say a waste of time because in a highly pragmatic world in which we are told that 'time is of the essence' any period not spent in work or activity or checking for the most recent text message or watching the preferred film courtesy of Netflix might be regarded as wasted. Time for prayer, time for reflection, for turning over the things of the day, for getting a perspective on what has happened, for rest, for sabbath – such time is in short supply. People where I live go to yoga classes as an activity to help them relax; it sounds more pragmatic, more businesslike, than saying, 'I think I'll sit down and be quiet for an hour.'

Yet these ancients and some of their contemporary successors would see down-time as a gift of love, when you offer your thoughts, your remembrances, your prayers for the well-being of the person whose life has touched yours.

Hence these two injunctions regarding prayers for the dead and dying:

Perform the prayers for the dead with fervour,
as if every one of the faithful who died
were a special friend of yours.
(St Columba, 6th century)

There is nothing that a man does on behalf of
the soul of one who dies that does not help it,
whether vigil or abstinence, or requiem or
frequent benedictions.
(The Rule of the Celi De, 6th century)

These acts of bereavement would be viewed by the ancients as being echoed in creation. For those who believe that all of life is interconnected, as we share the joy of a sunset so the rain shares the sorrow of our grief.

We find this reflected in a comment about Mael Anfaidh and a little bird.

Mael Anfaidh saw a certain little bird wailing and sorrowing. 'O God,' he said, 'what has happened here?'

An angel came towards him and said, 'Let it not trouble you any more. MoLua has died, and that is why living things bewail him, for he never killed a living thing, great or small. Men bewail his death no more than other living things among which is the little bird that you see.'

After my father died and his body had been cremated, my mother went on her own to scatter his ashes on a place where as young and older lovers they had often walked. It was beside a river. And my mother said that just as she had let his ashes go into the earth, a beautiful bird suddenly rose up from the waterside as if in tribute. And she felt blessed by this because my father was fond of birds.

When my mother died, my brothers and their partners and two

of my mother's close friends and I all went to the same riverside, and just after we had finished scattering her ashes, a beautiful Labrador dog suddenly bounded through long grass, ran in front of us and disappeared again. And there was no trace of an owner or family anywhere near it. And I remembered how my mother loved dogs.

I am not for a moment suggesting cause and effect – that somehow God has nothing more to do with his time than organise animals to appear when ashes are being scattered. That is much too mechanistic. There is something much more consoling about being open to the mystery of an interconnected world which shares joy and sorrow.

And perhaps if we were more attentive to the joy and sorrow, the beauty and pain which is present in and inflicted on nature, then perhaps we would find the natural world more commonly being in solidarity with us.

3) Death as continuation of a journey

The Celtic tradition – unlike some other traditions – does not regard human life as cyclical.

The world is cyclical, nature is cyclical … the earth goes round the sun, night follows day, and in nature there are seasons of budding, blossoming, withering and dying, all of which are repeated again and again.

But, though mortals may return to the earth from which they came, the Celts had a strong belief that when the energy to pursue the path of mortal life had ended, there was an energy within the soul to walk on, having cast off the weariness and burdens of humanity. This was in keeping with the traditions of pilgrimage which were alive and well in the early Celtic period and are being rediscovered in this new millennium.

People came on pilgrimage to Iona … journeying to a place

where prayer had been made, in the belief that whatever the destination might be, the journey there would have its own reward. All over Scotland there are similar places of pilgrimage, some of which are very focused. For example, in past centuries, people came from all over Europe to the small Orcadian island of Papa Westray in the hope of restoration of sight.

Indeed, when in a larger scale of things, people from the Celtic nations went on pilgrimage to Rome, there was a saying frequently brought to mind:

> *To go on pilgrimage to Rome*
> *is a fine thing.*
> *But the king whom you seek there*
> *you will not find*
> *unless you take him with you.*

Here is a poem and blessing which Carmichael collected regarding the journey of death:

> *Thou goest home this night to thy home of winter,*
> *to thy home of autumn, of spring, of summer;*
> *thou goest home this night to thy perpetual home*
> *to thine eternal bed, to thine eternal slumber.*
>
> *Sleep thou this night in the breast of thy Mother,*
> *sleep, thou beloved, while she herself soothes thee;*
> *sleep thou this night on the Virgin's arm,*
> *sleep, thou beloved, while she herself kisses thee.*
>
> *The shadow of death lies upon thy face, beloved,*
> *but the Jesus of grace has his hand around thee.*
> *In nearness to the Trinity bid farewell to thy pains;*
> *Christ stands before thee and peace is in his mind.*

Sleep in the calm of all calm,
sleep in the guidance of guidance,
sleep in the love of loves;
sleep, O beloved, in the Lord of life,
sleep, O beloved, in the God of life.[9]

Alexander Carmichael added a diary note to this poem. He said that death blessings (such as this) are known by different names such as Soul Leading or Soul Peace. They are intoned over the dying person, and the one who does this is called the Anam Chara or soul-friend. He or she is held in special affection for ever by the family and friends of the dying one.

The soul peace is sung slowly – with all present earnestly joining in – asking the Godhead to receive the departing soul. During the prayer, the soul-friend makes the sign of the cross with the right thumb over the lips of the dying one.

It is touching and striking in the extreme, says Carmichael, to see these lovable island people taking leave of those who are near and dear to them in their pilgrimage of crossing the river of death, the great ocean of darkness, the mountains of eternity.

The following text was originally sung to an island tune which would be played on the bagpipes and then sung. Carmichael records that on the island of Lewis:

the scene and the tune were singularly impressive – the moaning
of the sea, the mourning of the women, the lament of the pipes as
the body was carried to its home of winter, autumn, spring and
summer … and as nature seemed to join in the feelings of humanity.

I am going home with thee,
to thy home, to thy home.
I am going home with thee
to thy home of winter, autumn
spring and summer.

I am going home with thee,
thou child of my love,
to thy eternal bed,
to thy perpetual sleep. [10]

Because of our paucity of songs for the seasons of death and grieving, my colleagues and I have occasionally produced such material, often based on the legacy we inherit from our Celtic ancestors. Here are two of them, the first of which is really the versification of notes which I took from a young father who, with his wife, had recently sustained the loss of their first baby at birth. They had been told that she was lacking essential organs and that the rigour of birth would probably terminate her life. So they had her by Caesarean section and held her in their arms as she was baptised and died shortly thereafter.

Apart from her death, what grieved them was the lack of any text which articulated the very singular loss of a baby, where it is not the past which has been taken away, but the anticipated future.

We cannot care for you the way we wanted,
or cradle you, or listen for your cry;
but separated as we are by silence,
love will not die.

We cannot watch you growing into childhood
and find a new uniqueness every day.
But special as you would have been among us
you still will stay.

We cannot know the pain or the potential
which passing years would summon or reveal;
but for that true fulfilment Jesus promised
we hope and feel.

So, through the mess of anger, grief and tiredness,
through tensions which are not yet reconciled,
we give to God the worship of our sorrow
and our dear child.

Lord, in your arms which cradle all creation
we place our baby beyond death,
believing that she now, alive in heaven,
breathes with your breath. [11]

This second song is set to a tune called *The Iona Boat Song*. It is said to have been the tune to which the bodies of ancient kings of Scotland and other nations were piped across the water to their rest on Iona.

From the falter of breath,
through the silence of death,
to the wonder that's waiting beyond,
God has woven a way
unapparent by day
for all those of whom heaven is fond.

From frustration and pain,
through hope hard to sustain,
to the wholeness here promised, there known,
Christ has gone where we fear
and has vowed to be near
on the journey we make on our own.

From the dimming of light
through the darkness of night
to the glory of goodness above,
God the Spirit is sent
to ensure heaven's intent
is embraced and completed in love.

From today till we die,
through all questioning why,
to the place from which time and tide flow,
angels tread on our dreams
and magnificent themes
of heaven's promise are echoed below. [12]

4) The balancing time

As to what people expected after death, we cannot be altogether sure. There certainly was an anticipation of being in a bright place. There was the hope of fond reunions and intimacy with the saints, angels, God and Jesus.

The Celts, who were never affected by Augustinian notions of original sin, did not live so much with the fear of hell, damnation or limbo as other believers. But they did believe that there would be a time when we had to account for our lives – the Balancing Time. And I can say little more about that than what its title suggests. But because I believe it is better for all of us to embrace death rather than live in fear of it, I think that we have to find language for people today to somehow hold the mystery of the experience.

It must be 16 years or more ago when a friend of mine, a very diligent and caring pastor, phoned me in a dilemma. He was chaplain to a high school. The day before, he had learned that four teenagers from that school had all been killed in a car crash. One, perhaps two, were people of faith, two were not.

The school was going to assemble and he had no idea what he might say to this mixed group of grieving teenagers. So I sent him the following meditation which puts the much-feared mystery of death in the context of the better-loved mystery of birth.

I never wanted to be born.

The older I grew,
the fonder I became
of my mother's womb
and its warmth
and its safety,

I feared the unknown:
the next world
about which I knew nothing,
but imagined the worst.

Yet, as I grew older,
I sensed in my soul
that the womb was not my home forever.

Though I did not know when,
I felt sure that one day
I would disappear through a door
which had yet to be opened,
and confront the unknown
of which I was afraid.

And then,
it happened.

In blood, tears and pain,
it happened.

I was cut off from the familiar;
I left my life behind
and discovered …
not darkness, but light;
not hostility, but love;

not eternal separation,
but hands that wanted to hold me.

(Pause)

I never wanted to be born.

I don't want to die.

The older I grow,
the fonder I become
of this world
and its warmth
and its safety.

I fear the unknown:
the next world
about which I know nothing,
but imagine the worst.

Yet as I grow older,
I sense in my soul
that this world is not my home forever.

Though I do not know when,
I feel that one day
I will disappear through a door
which has yet to be opened.

Perhaps having come so safely through the first door,
I should not fear so hopelessly the second. [13]

There are two other codicils I'd like to add.

   One was the use – unique in Christian history, as far as I can understand – of verses 7-10 of Psalm 24:

Lift up your heads, you gates,
lift yourselves up, you everlasting doors,
that the king of glory may come in.
Who is this king of glory?
The Lord strong and mighty,
the Lord mighty in battle.

Lift up your heads, you gates,
lift them up, you everlasting doors,
that the king of glory may come in.
Who is he, the king of glory?
The Lord of Hosts, he is the king of glory.

In the Christian church, which has at times recognised in the Psalms a pre-figuring of Christ's ministry, this text has, through the ages, been associated with a number of things:

The opening up of the gates to the earth at the incarnation
The opening up of Jerusalem's gates on Palm Sunday
The opening up of the gates of death at the Resurrection
The opening up of the gates to heaven at the Ascension

But for the ancient Celts in the 7th century, this text was read on Holy Saturday, the eve of Easter Day, when the church remembered Christ descending to the dead to harrow hell and release those souls whom Satan held in captivity. For them it was an image of consolation symbolising that no one, for whatever reason they had gone or been led astray, would languish in hell for ever. Jesus was their liberator.

And finally, here is a lovely image of heaven which comes – some say – from St Brigid in the 6th century, while others place it in 14th-century Ireland. It is certainly a woman's poem and highly offensive to people who are teetotallers.

The Heavenly Banquet

I would like to have the men of heaven
in my own house
with barrels of good cheer
laid out for them

I would like to have the three Marys ...
their fame is so great;
I would like people
from every corner of Heaven.

I would like them to be cheerful
in their drinking.
I would like to have Jesus too
here among them.

I would like a great lake of beer
for the King of Kings.
I would like to be watching Heaven's family
drinking it through all eternity.

1   Anne Gordon: *Candle for the Foundling* (Pentland Press) p481
2   Anne Gordon: Op Cit p482
3   Alice Roberts: *The Celts* (Heron Books) Chapter 1
4   Alastair McIntosh: *Soil and Soul* (Aurum Press) pp233-235
5   Alexander Carmichael: *Carmina Gadelica* (Floris Books) no 327
6   Alexander Carmichael Op Cit no 328
7   Alexander Carmichael Op Cit no 330
8   George MacLeod: *The Whole Earth Shall Cry Glory* (Wild Goose Publications) p24
9   Alexander Carmichael Op Cit no 346
10 Alexander Carmichael Op Cit no 345

11 John L Bell & Graham Maule: *The Last Journey* (Wild Goose Publications) p88

12 John L Bell & Graham Maule: Op Cit p66

13 John L Bell: *He Was In The World* (Wild Goose Publications) p18

Licence to age

The Duke of Edinburgh is to be congratulated on his decision to give up his driving licence, because in doing so he allows millions of other people in their senior years to follow his example and consider what changes in lifestyle would be for their benefit and that of others.

This is not a broadside against older people. Not at all. Indeed it riles me when in print or in parliament we are warned of the difficulties of Britain having an 'ageing population'. The very phrase is tautologous. Every living individual and every nation under the sun is ageing. It's part of being alive. We can't avoid it.

A newborn baby is ageing at exactly the same rate as her grannie. We don't stay in our diapers for ever. Ageing is a sign of growth, not an existential indictment.

The truth is that far more of us live longer than our predecessors did, largely due to a succession of advances in medicine and social care. But if society laments growing older, religious communities have to maintain, from a biblical perspective, that old age comes with great expectations.

At the very start of the history of the three Abrahamic faiths – Judaism, Christianity and Islam – is the story of an old man aged a hundred called Abraham and his ninety-year-old wife called Sarah who are told by God to go on a journey and start a new nation.

Indeed in the Christmas season, now long past, God calls another retired couple – Elizabeth and Zechariah – to be accomplices in the new thing God is doing.

This is the vocation on us as we grow older: not to cling to positions of power, responsibility or status until we die, wary of letting anyone younger take our place. Rather, as we grow older, we should recognise what we no longer need to do, give that up and use our energy to enable and encourage those who come after us.

Since I was very young I always looked for an older person I could emulate. Even yet. Two days ago I had a fascinating conversation over dinner with a young lady in her early eighties. I hope I am as generous and politically astute when I am her age. Last month I danced in a friend's kitchen with his mother-in-law who is in her nineties. I hope I will be as supple and positive when I am her age.

But one thing I will not do is emulate the Duke of Edinburgh by giving up my driving licence – for the simple reason that I've never had one.

Thought for the Day
11 February 2019

Choices for living

As an occasional visitor to the National Portrait Gallery in London, I was interested to hear that this significant and politically neutral establishment should be inciting controversy.

The issue concerns a number of artists who have written to the Gallery's director suggesting that it should sever its ties with British Petroleum, one of its major sponsors, on the grounds that oil giants contribute more to the problem of climate change than to its solution, a charge which BP is keen to deny.

Sponsorship can be controversial. Whether it is the defence industry funding research in our universities, or fast-food giants sponsoring sporting events, the donation of millions of pounds seems like a magnanimous gesture which, for many people, is good reason for compliment rather than criticism.

As regards the Portrait Gallery, it might be claimed that its troublesome artists are biting the hand that feeds them when they suggest that the Gallery should be selective in responding to the beneficence of donors.

This issue was put in perspective for me by something which happened three weeks ago when I was working in New Zealand. It was a conference of head teachers and senior pupils from Anglican schools, including participants from Tonga, Samoa and Fiji. On the last day, I was conducting a seminar on the relationship between Christian faith and the environment. To start it off, I invited the thirty or so pupils to sit among adults in the audience. I asked them to tell the adults how they foresaw the future, and then listen as the adults told them when they first became aware of the issue of climate change. I gave them fifteen minutes to speak and listen to each other.

After that conversation, I asked the adults if they might indicate anything surprising that they had heard from the teenagers.

One woman said, 'I was shocked to hear one of the pupils say that the threats to the environment made her unsure as to whether she should marry or have children if the world's future is so unstable.' The girl in question came from Fiji which has already been badly affected by climate change. For her, as for all Christians, the care of creation is not an option, but a divine mandate which can involve the sacrifice of self-interest – something which lies at the core of the Christian faith.

It seems to me that when we are faced with a climate crisis which the economist and Nobel Laureate Joseph Stiglitz has called 'our world war', there is dignity in those who make choices they know may be to their personal cost. Such decisions are measures of love and concern, and a feature of responsible living.

Thought for the Day
11 June 2019

The significance of symbols

This is not an academic thesis, but a personal reflection on the power and purpose of symbols and symbolic action.

We humans are highly symbolic beings, though we sometimes live in denial of that. It becomes clear when we think of the implications of how a symbol is a means of representing a reality greater than itself.

The most common symbols we use are words, especially nouns. These are the first words we teach children. They learn 'mum' and 'dad' or 'dog' or 'cow' and associate these words with particular people and animals. We don't teach them verbs, adjectives or adverbs first. These will come later. The early nouns are signs of the reality they point to. No one ever tells us this; we learn by experience.

When we see the word 'chocolate' we don't immediately eat the word, because we know instinctively that it is only a verbal symbol which describes an enjoyable reality.

Pre-literate societies had sophisticated languages, even if the words were not written down. Ancient European cave paintings and the fascinating dot paintings of Australian Aboriginal tribes show how non-verbal symbols enabled people to record moments in tribal history which could only be understood by those who shared a comprehension of what the symbols represented. In more sophisticated societies, the Morse code and semaphore signalling are two examples of how meaning is communicated without words to those who understand the specialised symbolic vocabulary.

But on a more personal level, symbols and symbolic action have a profound significance, the value or even the existence of which is only understood when the symbol or action is broken or breached. Here are some examples:

1) A child always kisses his or her grandmother when they meet. But one day, and for no apparent reason, the child refuses to kiss the grandmother. So the grandmother becomes concerned regarding why this usual mark of affection has not been shown.

2) A husband and wife might have blazing arguments with each other, which often end with the wife slamming a door and going to bed. But on a given occasion she does something very different. Instead of shouting and vacating the shared space, she takes the wedding ring off her finger and throws it into the rubbish bin. The husband does not know what to do.

3) A respected teacher in a British school, who previously had been in the army, always on the week before Remembrance Sunday wears a red poppy in his lapel. He is the only teacher who does this. But one year, disgusted by the extent of British weapons sales to ruthless dictatorships he decides, without speaking about it, to wear a white peace poppy instead. His pupils and fellow teachers do not understand.

In each case, when the symbol or symbolic action is changed or omitted, a truth is alluded to without the use of words.

We should not be surprised at human symbolic activity because we are the children of a God who consistently in Scripture delights in initiating or encouraging symbolic action, though we don't always recognise it.

a) The rainbow in the sky is not a symbol of new-age spirituality, but of God's decision to put his weapon of war (the bow is a weapon) out of reach by hanging it in the sky, so that all creatures might see how seriously God takes the covenant made between heaven and earth. (*Genesis 9:12-14*)

b) When crossing the Jordan, each of the Hebrew tribes is requested to lift a stone from the river bed to be turned into a commemorative cairn which symbolises the graciousness of God to the itinerant community. *(Joshua 4:1-8)*

c) Jeremiah buys a field in a war zone to symbolise that no matter how bleak the future may seem, God will not give up on the nation or on the city of Jerusalem. *(Jeremiah 32:6-15)*

d) Jesus, in accepting the anointing of his head with expensive perfume, identifies this act as symbolic of preparing his body for burial. *(Matthew 26:6-13)*

e) In heaven, those invited to the wedding feast of the Lamb are appropriately dressed in fine and shining linen. The fine linen signifies the righteous deeds of God's people. *(Revelation 19:5-8)*

Essential as symbols are in human life and in holy Scripture, the post-Reformation churches have sometimes been wary of them. There was a perception by Lutheran and Calvinist reformers that the hyper-ornate nature of pre-Reformation liturgy had become more important than the Gospel call on people's lives. The continuation of these vacuous ritual acts had to be terminated.

In some countries, of which Scotland was one, the reformers were iconoclasts. They broke religious artifacts – stained glass, statuary or paintings; they removed crosses from churches, and burned music manuscripts in an attempt to create a 'purer' church more worthy of being called the Bride of Christ.

Out went the cruciform shape of churches, the prominence of the holy table, the side chapels; and out went the Latin liturgy and choral singing. The focus of attention moved architecturally from the celebrant at the east-end altar, to the preacher in the pulpit which was sometimes physically moved to a central position on the north or south wall of the repurposed building. And where biblical symbols – the lamb, the vine, the river, the crown of thorns – had once adorned the walls, now all might be painted white, though occasionally biblical texts, especially the Ten Commandments or the Apostles' Creed, would be allowed as the sole decorative distraction from the spoken words of the pastor.

For many people of my (post-war) generation, this puritanical sensibility was evident in our churches in the mid-20th century. In my childhood, there was no Advent wreath, no lit candles (it was presumed that John Calvin had invented the electric light), no visibility of the baptismal font most Sundays, no colours on the clerical dress unless the minister was bold enough to wear an academic hood. The prevailing opinion was that symbols were 'Catholic', meaning Roman Catholic. It never dawned on us that this abhorrence of symbols and symbolic action was itself highly symbolic. The barren aesthetic suggested that God disdained anything other than the preached word, as if intellectual engagement was all, as if membership of Christ's kingdom had to do with mental thought and a knowledge of the right answers.

Rather than be abstract, I want to briefly relate three incidents which convinced me of the importance of symbolism.

St Mary's Episcopal Cathedral, Glasgow

I had never been in a church building other than of the Calvinist variety until Holy Week in 1969 when I was studying at Glasgow University. The nearest church building to my residence was the Episcopal Cathedral. I noted it had a Maundy Thursday evening service and went along. I had never been in such a formal liturgical setting – a robed choir, responsive prayers, the eucharist served at the altar rather than to people sitting in pews.

It came to the end of the service and Psalm 22 was read responsively by a solo lector and the congregation. While this happened, the choir took off their robes. They then began to douse all the candles and to carry out of the building anything of beauty or significance – the altar cloths, chairs, the cross, and other small furnishings and fabric. It was done in a mad rush and all the while we kept reading the psalm antiphonally as the lights dimmed. At the end of the psalm few people could see to read the text. When the last light went out, the lector, quoting Jesus, said:

> *'I will smite the shepherd*
> *and the sheep will be scattered.'*

… and then everyone quickly left the building in silence.

I felt as if I had abandoned Jesus, like the disciples in Gethsemane. It wasn't acting. It was pure Scripture, the impact of which was amplified by the power of responsible symbolic action.

Liturgy course, Glasgow

Move on fifteen years, by which time I was ordained and running a course on music and worship with my colleague. We had around sixty people on each of six evenings and we always ended with a short liturgy. One evening, we decided that the liturgy would focus on Jesus as the Light of life, the Word made flesh, and the Saviour of the world.

After a preliminary song and prayer we read some words from the Bible appropriate to these three titles given to Christ. As the words were spoken, someone laid on the long central table around which we were gathered three objects – a large lit candle, a Bible and a cross. My colleague then suggested that rather than pray aloud, we might like to think of people who needed to have the Light of Christ shine on them, or the Word of God move them, or the Saviour of the world forgive them.

With much daring, we had acquired from a Roman Catholic bookshop small votive candles, and my colleague suggested that people might, if they wished, take one, light it and put it beside whichever of the three symbols – large candle, Bible or cross – was appropriate. We began to sing a chant: *Kindle a flame to lighten the dark, and take all fear away.*

I was playing the piano and could not see what was happening, but I sensed that a number of people were leaving their seats to go towards the table. By the end, as if it were an artwork, there was a single line of votive lights which went from the large candle at one end of the table, over the open Bible in the middle and around the cross at the other end.

The next day I was in a bookshop where a deacon of the church stopped me to say that a member of her congregation had been at the workshop the night before and was telling everyone of how she – a diehard Protestant – had lit a candle for the first time in her life. It was for her son who was in prison on a murder charge, and the action had been so important for her. The woman in question would never have uttered a vocal prayer in public, but she could pray through the symbol.

North Shore Methodist Church, Chicago

I went to this church with a Roman Catholic colleague who worked for our North American publishers. If I stayed with him over a weekend we would always go to a different denominational church on Sunday.

The Methodist church was oblong in shape, and as you entered it the whole congregation saw you, because the main door was facing the congregation rather than behind it. We were last in and the building was packed. My colleague Mike entered first, saw a large circular baptismal font and immediately went over to it, put his fingers in the water and blessed himself. I was horrified, but said nothing.

After the service when we were having coffee, I asked him why he had 'done that with the water in the font in front of all these people', and he replied. 'Are you ashamed of your baptism?'

Until that moment I had always presumed that the act of crossing or blessing yourself was a superstitious Roman Catholic gesture to ward off evil. I never knew that in touching the water he was affirming his status as a baptised believer, and claiming his membership in the Body of Christ irrespective of the denomination.

In the work I have been engaged in over the past forty years, with teenagers and adults alike, I have found that the responsible use of symbols and symbolic action speaks to the souls of people in a way in which the logic of argument or the emotion of music seldom does.

For forty years I have asked lay people in workshops and conferences to identify what has been a significant worship experience for them. Only twice in hundreds of occasions has someone mentioned a sermon, and on both occasions it was a pastor remembering one of the former princes of the pulpit. This is not to discount preaching; it is my primary vocation. But it is to say that the Holy Spirit is not operative through words alone. God is more than the Lord of the intellect.

I have used the word 'responsible' with regard to symbolic action on two occasions and this is deliberate, because there are places where gimmickry has masqueraded as symbolic action, and turned liturgy into an entertainment exercise rather than a devotional experience. It might help if I indicate three associated but not synonymous terms.

A **gimmick** always points to itself. Blowing up a balloon and letting it go was, in one cathedral I attended, allegedly a symbolic action to remind us of the activity of the Holy Spirit at Pentecost. It was not. It was an amusing distraction to make children smile, nothing more. A gimmick points only to itself.

A **sign** has only one function which is to point to a specific entity beyond itself. A sign saying 'exit' does not lead us to the toilets or the cafe. It points simply to where we can leave the building.

A **symbol** invites us to ponder a deep truth of which it is the emblem. The stones from the middle of the river Jordan which the Hebrews heaped together was not a carefully crafted architectural monument; it was a pile of material from the river bed to symbolise how God had brought the people through deep waters. The wine which we sip in the eucharist is not offered so that we can guess its provenance, but to enable us to ponder the generosity, forgiveness and grace of God.

A gimmick and a sign will always mean the same to all who are engaged with them, but a symbol opens up realms of thought, wonder and devotion which may variously affect different people. Symbols and symbolic action, like Scripture itself, are not shallow but profound.

Travelling mercies

The first time I heard the phrase 'travelling mercies' it conjured up the image of a good book and a glass of red wine in a first class compartment on the journey home to Glasgow. However, I don't think the person who last week prayed that I might receive 'travelling mercies' had these delights in mind.

It's a phrase from the 19th century, originally used to ask a blessing on people who were going on long and arduous missionary journeys. More recently it has come into the public domain as the title of a book by Anne Lamott.

It might be a pertinent thing to pray or wish for today, at this very hour when many train travellers in England will be discovering the novelties of the revised timetable, especially if the usual train no longer calls at their station or the number of trains has been cut, or the journey time has been lengthened.

Train travel used to be a pleasant experience. I remember in previous decades boarding the 7 o'clock from Glasgow to London on which most people would be catching up on sleep or digesting the newspapers.

When I travelled on that train recently, it was like a business office with people typing assiduously on their laptops, men sitting opposite each other having a pre-meeting conversation; and others on their mobile phones discussing everything from the Dow Jones index to Italian restaurants in the capital which serve gluten-free tagliatelle. All this at 07.00. It makes you wonder how the nation survived when travel time was travel time and work began when you got there.

It seems to me that life is not enhanced if a journey through the spring countryside in the company of other human beings becomes little more than an inconvenience interrupting the flow of business. Are we becoming so driven by other people's agendas that daydreaming and silently musing have become suspect activities?

There is, of course, no biblical advice regarding relaxing train travel or the nuisance of changed timetables. But I'm drawn to the story in the Hebrew scriptures of Jacob going on a journey, falling asleep en route, and having a dream of angels ascending and descending a stairway to heaven.

If this morning's travellers can't be given that travelling mercy, maybe they can dream about a good book and a glass of wine on the journey home.

Thought for the Day
21 May 2018

Wild Goose Publications, the publishing house of the Iona Community established in the Celtic Christian tradition of Saint Columba, produces books, e-books, CDs and digital downloads on:

- holistic spirituality
- social justice
- political and peace issues
- healing
- innovative approaches to worship
- song in worship, including the work of the Wild Goose Resource Group
- material for meditation and reflection

For more information:

Wild Goose Publications
The Iona Community
Suite 9, Fairfield, 1048 Govan Road
Glasgow G51 4XS, Scotland

Tel. +44 (0)141 429 7281
e-mail: admin@ionabooks.com

or visit our website at
www.ionabooks.com
for details of all our products and online sales

For more information about the Wild Goose Resource Group:
www.wildgoose.scot